THE FORGOTTEN CHARGE

THE 123RD PENNSYLVANIA AT MARYE'S HEIGHTS, FREDERICKSBURG, VIRGINIA

By
Scott B. Lang

D1508857

WHITE MANE BOOKS
SHIPPENSBURG, PENNSYLVANIA

All maps were created by the author.

This White Mane Books publication
was printed by
Beidel Printing House, Inc.
63 West Burd Street
Shippensburg, PA 17257-0708 USA

The acid-free paper used in this book meets the guidelines for permanence and durability of the Committee on Production Guidelines for Book Longevity of the Council on Library Resources.

For a complete list of available publications
please write
White Mane Books
Division of White Mane Publishing Company, Inc.
P.O. Box 708
Shippensburg, PA 17257-0708 USA

Library of Congress Cataloging-in-Publication Data

Lang, Scott B., 1956-
   The forgotten charge : the 123rd Pennsylvania at Marye's Heights, Fredericksburg,
Virginia / by Scott B. Lang.
      p. cm.
   Includes bibliographical references and index.
   ISBN 1-57249-292-9 (alk. paper)
   1. Fredericksburg (Va.), Battle of, 1862. 2. United States. Army. Pennsylvania Infantry
Regiment, 123rd (1862-1865) 3. United States--History--Civil War,
1861-1865--Regimental histories. 4. Pennsylvania--History--Civil War,
1861-1865--Regimental histories. I. Title.

E474.85 .L364 2002
973.7'33--dc21

                                                                              2002023487

To Laura and Alfred, my inspiration from the past
and
To Leslie and Chris, my inspiration of today

CONTENTS

ILLUSTRATIONS AND MAPS

PREFACE

The year is the one-hundredth anniversary of the conclusion of the Civil War. A small, 93-year-old woman sits with children at her feet, telling the many stories of her father's exploits during the war. She sadly relates how all of the old soldiers are now gone, and with them, their many tales of the conflict. She cannot help but wonder if these stories will be forgotten.

The young children show little interest in what she has to tell. Many wander off to other parts of the house to explore previously unknown corners. Others only half-listen to her accounts, solely in deference to her age, not because of what she is saying. None realize that the opportunity to hear these stories will soon be lost with her passing.

I was one such lad who did not listen intently when my great-grandmother told the tales of her father. I wish today I had. For some of her stories, even though hearsay, could have been told in these very pages. But I was only nine years old and had other, more important things to do.

When I undertook the task of writing about my great-great-grandfather's regiment, I could not help but think that some of the stories did, in fact, stick with me. As I grew older, I became increasingly more interested in his unit due, in part, to the tales of my great-grandmother. I began researching the regiment. The more I found, the more I wanted to know. In the end, I felt that the story of these extraordinary men had to be told.

So to my great-grandmother who tried to pass on the legacy, I can only say that I really did listen. To her and the men of the 123rd Pennsylvania, I can only hope, in a very small way, that I have made you proud.

INTRODUCTION

It has often been said that the winner of a war has the privilege of writing its history. The truth of this statement can readily be seen in the paucity of work that has been written regarding the battles of Fredericksburg and Chancellorsville. While a number of books and articles have been written that tell the rather disappointing stories of these contests, the total amount of work does not compare to the volumes written about the other, more successful campaigns.

But the word "successful" is important in the understanding of this shortage of published works. The period from December of 1862 until May of 1863 was not a shining moment for the Union army in the East. During this time, the Army of Northern Virginia had decisively defeated its Northern adversary in the major battles that had been fought. These losses were so total and unequivocal that many began to earnestly question whether the North had the resolve to win the war. This newfound pessimism was present in the Northern press. The growing embarrassment over these defeats caused Northern journalists to write less about these contests in exchange for more glowing tales of the Union's successes in other regions. As the war neared the end, these contests were pushed back even further in the public's consciousness. Suffice it to say, even to this day, these battles have not received the exposure of other eastern battles.

In the case of Fredericksburg, the shortage of work is even more striking than the rather limited amount of work related to Chancellorsville. While some books provide the strategy, or lack of strategy in this contest, few tell the story from the soldier's

perspective. To the soldiers, this was a battle which could ultimately right the losing ways of the Army of the Potomac. The
men in blue charged valiantly against a nearly impregnable position and never wavered in their duty to their army and their country. Yet interestingly enough, the stories of these men have rarely
been told.

Scarcely six months later a group of men attacked another
entrenched line at the pivotal Battle of Gettysburg. Although the
uniform color had changed, the result of this ill-fated charge was
the same as its earlier counterpart. It is no wonder that the Union
soldiers, after repulsing this attack, yelled "Fredericksburg . . .
Fredericksburg" at their unsuccessful adversaries. As the years
moved on, this attack took on the character as the penultimate
charge in the Civil War. Books and articles have been written in
which this attack appears almost mythical. While it is difficult to
determine how many pages have been written about "Pickett's
Charge," more has clearly been written about it than about the
charge at Frederickburg.

How did this happen? As early as 1869, writers began to
argue that the charge at Fredericksburg was a more difficult charge
than Pickett's attack. General J. Watts DePeyster wrote: "At the
first Battle of Fredericksburg, the [Army of the Potomac's] determined bravery far transcended the fiery courage of the 'Army of
Northern Virginia,' its four years-long antagonist, as the difficulties that the former strove to overcome on the Rappahannock
exceeded those which the latter undertook to conquer at
Gettysburg."[1]

Other commentators were more tempered in their views but
still regarded the charge on Marye's Heights as equal to its latter
rival. State Senator Alexander K. McClure, in his dedication
speech for the Humphreys monument at Fredericksburg, noted:
"Only what were accepted as supreme military necessities made
Pickett's charge at Gettysburg and Humphreys' charge at
Fredericksburg, but they both stand in history, and will ever stand,
as high-water marks of the heroism of American soldiery."[2] This
author does not have the answer, nor wishes to argue one way or

another on the heroism of either group or contend that one charge was the more valiant attack. For in truth, both attacks possess unique qualities. But it is hard to argue that if the charge at Fredericksburg was anywhere near as valiant as its Gettysburg counterpart, these men have received their proper due. Too little has been written about these men and their attack that cold December day. Hopefully, this work can, at the very least, add a few more pages to the much-neglected history of these long forgotten common soldiers.

One such group of common soldiers heralded from Pittsburgh, Pennsylvania, and its surroundings, and formed what would later become known as the 123rd Pennsylvania Volunteer Infantry. These men would leave the relative safety of their homes in August of 1862 and come face to face with their destinies on the fields outside of Fredericksburg and Chancellorsville.

This relatively unknown regiment was recruited in July of 1862 by a Presbyterian minister from Allegheny City, a small town opposite Pittsburgh. This man of the cloth had been known to preach from the pulpit about the honorability of the Union cause. His adamant belief in the abolition of slavery was tempered by his understanding that men had to die in order to eradicate the deplorable institution. As Reverend John Barr Clark once eloquently told his parishioners: "Many a gallant son must die without the comfortable surroundings of home. But be not discouraged, the Lord of Peace is on our side."[3]

When the men of his congregation resolved to enlist and form a company, Reverend Clark quickly enrolled in the unit. He actively recruited for the company and in less than 36 hours, the minister-turned-soldier registered over two hundred "Christian patriots" for military duty. In less than two weeks, his organizational efforts had successfully created an entire regiment. For his efforts, Reverend Clark was unanimously elected the colonel of this new unit.

The regiment would move quickly to the field and be brigaded with three other newly formed Pennsylvania regiments. None of these four thousand men had ever seen battle. Three of the regiments, including the 123rd, would only enlist for nine months.

The story of this brigade, and more specifically of the 123rd, is constructed from a number of different sources. Two diaries from men in the 123rd paint an intimate day-to-day portrait of the group's varied marches and battles. Additional diaries and writings from the other regiments within the brigade help to relate the story of the days leading up to the group's baptism of fire.

By far, the most important source of information was obtained from the Pittsburgh newspapers that took an active interest in the 123rd. More than 125 articles have been consulted to relate the tale of the regiment as seen through the eyes of the participants and the newspaper reporters of the day. Some of these articles are being printed for the first time in this work.

These various sources reveal a somewhat similar story of the joys and heartaches of war. Since the regiment was initially formed in the basement of a church, many men joined out of love for God. Others enlisted out of devotion to their country. No matter why each man enlisted, the nine months that these soldiers spent in the field proved to be a test of each man's ideals.

Lack of supplies and constant marching tested the very core of the men's resolve. From the forced march to the battlefield at Antietam until their final fight at Chancellorsville, the men fought for their God and country. Although at some intervals the men would question the Union war effort and the military's resolve to win, they were always ready to answer the call to battle.

It is difficult to understand why the participation of these men in major battles has received such little attention in our modern discussion of the war. This work attempts to right that apparent historical oversight and give these men their rightful place in Civil War history.

CHAPTER ONE
HISTORICAL BACKGROUND

In the Beginning . . .

The first 15 months of the Civil War had hardly been a resounding victory for the Union cause. In truth, the Union army in the East had failed miserably in its attempts to end the war quickly. In March, April, and May of 1862, the army lost over 15,000 men in General George B. McClellan's attempt to attack Richmond from the Virginia peninsula. Even worse, during the Peninsula Campaign, the government had ceased all recruiting efforts. This, coupled with the recent losses, led to a shortage of men.

After much discussion, a new call for 300,000 volunteers was issued on July 2, 1862. This 300,000 figure was apportioned among all Northern states, based on their size, and Pennsylvania was informed that its quota was 21 regiments, or 21,000 men. The renewed call required each recruit to enlist for a three-year period.

Governor Andrew G. Curtin of Pennsylvania saw the problems inherent in this new allocation for volunteers. Pennsylvania, one of the larger states, would undoubtedly have difficulty in fulfilling its quota for three-year volunteers. Local recruiting groups informed the governor that they would only be able to raise the much-needed men if the term of enlistment was shortened. Consequently, the governor used his considerable political clout to convince the Lincoln administration that Pennsylvania be permitted to meet a portion of its quota with a number of nine-month regiments. After an initial denial by the Lincoln administration, the nine-month regiments were permitted to be mustered into military service.[1]

According to government records, the new enlistment rules proved extremely successful. By the end of 1862, 421,000 men had volunteered for three years of service and 88,000 for nine months of service.[2] Almost 16,000 of these short-term enlistees came from Pennsylvania. Of these recruits, one thousand were from the Pittsburgh area, and they evolved into what eventually became known as the 123rd Pennsylvania Volunteer Infantry. Two other units were recruited from other parts of Pennsylvania and became closely associated with the 123rd.

Initially, veterans questioned the patriotism of any individual who signed up for only nine months. Some asserted that the motivating factor for enlistment in these regiments had been the bounty. Others contended that these men were unhealthy and useless to the army. One newspaper went so far as to call these enlistees "Nine Months' Beauties." Needless to say, these disparaging comments led to a number of heated exchanges. In the *Pittsburgh Gazette* on March 17, 1863, a "'nine months' beauty" of the 123d Pennsylvania answered the allegations:

> . . . the reading of a piece in the Pittsburgh *Chronicle*, written by its special correspondent from Philadelphia, a person would be led to think that a certain class of soldiers, whom he denominated as "nine months' beauties," were not entitled to even the name of respectable citizens, and much less that of patriots, for he says that they brought "neither health, patriotism nor honesty into the army." Now, as for the healthiness, I appeal to any unprejudiced mind if, since the breaking out of the rebellion, there has left the city of Pittsburgh a finer or healthier set of men than the 123d Regiment? And I assert—and were it necessary, could give proof for my assertion—that the physicians' reports of sickness in the six regiments of the "nine months' beauties" in our division will stand favorably along with that of any other six regiments in the corps.[3]

In most communities, rallies were set up to help the recruiting process. Pittsburgh and its sister city, Allegheny City, proved no exception. On July 25, 1862, a rally was held in the West Commons of Allegheny City to arouse the public to enlist. This rally was well attended by Allegheny County residents—over 15,000 people were there. Many leading citizens gave speeches admonishing attendees to "[r]emember some of your friends and neighbors, in their full courage have fallen in the midst of battle."[4] While the meeting definitely aroused some of the war spirit that was felt during the war's early months, the overall enlistment response by those who attended was lukewarm.

Similar to most regiments of the time, the 123rd Pennsylvania was not initially recruited as a regiment. During the Civil War era, a regiment consisted of 10 companies. Each company had approximately one hundred members, thereby bringing the total number in a regiment to one thousand men.

Historically, the recruiting of a company commenced when a leading citizen of the community began to solicit members for his unit. In most circumstances, the individual who recruited the company was also the captain of the group. As companies began to fill, a regiment was created out of the companies that were being recruited from a given area. The 123rd was no exception.

The newspaper reports for the end of July and the beginning of August 1862 contain a number of references to individuals who attempted to raise a company. Horatio K. Tyler, a young man whom many remembered as the first librarian of the local library, actively recruited men for his unit. Hugh Danver, a butcher, put together a unit from the butchers in his

Horatio K. Tyler

This librarian-turned-soldier became the commander of Company D and a soldier of extraordinary ability.

Under the Maltese Cross

locale. David E. Adams, a father of four and a blacksmith, approached all the "elite young mechanics" in the city to join his company.[5]

Even with all of the above-mentioned men actively seeking members, the overall recruiting effort in Allegheny County still proceeded at a relatively slow pace during July 1862. The *Pittsburgh Dispatch* summarized the recruiting results as of August 1:

> John Watt Infantry—Thomas Maxwell, recruiting officer; sixty men. Headquarters 400 Liberty Street.
>
> Howe Engineers, D. E. Adams, recruiting officer; twenty men. Headquarters Town Hall, Allegheny.
>
> Cass Infantry, Capt. A. Gast, recruiting officer; twenty-nine men. Headquarters Diamond, Allegheny.
>
> Allegheny Infantry, Richard C. Dale, recruiting officer; twenty-five men. Headquarters No. 104 Federal Street, Allegheny.
>
> Butchers' Infantry, H. Danver, recruiting officer; twenty-five men. Headquarters Marks Store, Allegheny.[6]

As a result, after the first few weeks of recruiting, the companies that became part of the 123rd had only mustered 159 men. This tepid response suddenly changed on August 5, 1862, when Reverend John Barr Clark, a 32-year-old presbyterian minister in Allegheny City, began his recruitment for "Christian patriots."

Reverend Clark was a relatively new minister to Allegheny City in the summer of 1862. He arrived in the city during the fall of 1860 and had held his post as the minister of the 2nd United Presbyterian Church of Allegheny for less than two years. However, in this short time, Reverend Clark's congregation had come to know that their minister was a strong advocate for the abolition of slavery and the preservation of the Union. He also made it abundantly clear that he understood that men had to die in order to protect these cherished ideals. As he later wrote in a letter from the field:

> Fellow citizens, you have had many sacrifices during this bloody war. You have given your sons to confront the enemy

on the field of battle. You have given your money to furnish
the implements of war. But the day of sacrifice has not expired. Many a field must yet be reddened with human gore.
Many a gallant son must die without the comfortable surroundings of home. But be not discouraged, the Lord of Peace
is on our side. He will reward you for all these sacrifices,
and fill the land with peace. God speed the day when war
shall cease and when the whole earth shall be filled with His
glory, who is the prince of peace.[7]

Reverend John Barr Clark

The colonel and spiritual leader of the
123rd.

Under the Maltese Cross

**•ATTENTION! CHRISTIAN PA-
TRIOTS.**—All persons desiring t join a company of Nine Months' Volunteers, under the command
of REV. J. R. CLARK, can have an opportunity of
doing so by calling at the store of JAMES CALDWELL,
Federal street, Allegheny, during the remaining
days of this week. Any person from a distance wish-
ing to go can address me, Box 114 Allegheny, Pa., or
call at my residence, No. 19 North Common.
aug6:3t   JOHN R. CLARK.

Reverend Clark's call for "Christian Patriots" on
August 8, 1862.

Pittsburgh Gazette

During the early weeks of July, Reverend Clark appears not to have taken an active role in recruiting. He was not mentioned as a speaker in any of the early meetings. A number of other presbyterian ministers, namely Reverend James Priestly and Reverend William D. Howard, were prominently mentioned in the early recruiting rallies. Clark's lack of involvement changed on August 5, 1862, when a reporter wrote:

> On Tuesday evening (August 5) I witnessed a scene that inspired me with more hope than anything I have seen for a long time. Taking a walk along the South Common, in Allegheny, I heard some animated speaking in the lecture room of the 2d United Presbyterian Church. I took the liberty to walk in and found that it was a war meeting. The young men of the congregation had met to organize a volunteer company, to be led by their pastor, the Rev. J. B. Clark, as their captain. After a short and business like discussion, Mr. Clark, who was present, enrolled his name, and was followed instantly and enthusiastically by many of the young gentleman present, having a very good beginning.[8]

The young men who enlisted on this day were clearly of strong moral fiber. Due to the moral quality of Clark's men, the reporter believed that his company would fill quickly. As such, he strongly recommended that any man who wished to serve with a group of moral men, rather than a "company of rude and profane men," should promptly enlist. The reporter concluded his article with one final endorsement: "[T]hink . . . of the influence for good on thousands that can be exerted by a solid mass of one hundred intelligent Christian men, led by a strong and warm hearted minister of the Gospel, who fights for his country, his God and Truth."[9]

The editor's observations proved prophetic. The desire to be a part of this unit was so strong that the initial company was filled in a matter of 36 hours. Thereafter, two more companies were recruited by the reverend. One of these companies would be led by the mayor of Allegheny City, Simon Drum.

This spiritual awakening precipitated by Reverend Clark clearly invigorated enlistment in the Allegheny County area. The August 8 edition of the *Pittsburgh Dispatch* summarized the progress of each of the local companies. Captain Danver of the Butcher's Infantry had 130 men on his muster roll and began forming a second company with the surplus. Reverend Clark had 160 recruits and was also forming a second company. Captains Frederick Gast, Tyler, and David E. Adams each reported close to one hundred men.[10] Reverend Clark's influence was undeniably felt, as the regiment went from 159 members to 594 in one short week.

The next few weeks were important in the development of the 123rd. The independent companies that were formed by other individuals were slowly being absorbed into Reverend Clark's unit. Two companies arrived in Pittsburgh from Tarentum, a small industrial city in northeastern Allegheny County, and joined forces with the men of Clark's congregation. By the middle of August, a regimental size unit was put together solely from Allegheny County men. It was no wonder that Reverend Clark became its colonel.

The men who ultimately comprised these companies were a spattering of young and old, rich and poor. Samuel Taggart, a 21-year-old first sergeant in Company H, was a recent graduate from Westminster College. Alfred Masonhimer, a 21-year-old painter, was only married for one day when he joined his company. Joseph Park, a sergeant in Company E, was a 26-year-old druggist. Henry F. Eggers, an 18-year-old private in Company H, was a farmer from Snowden Township. Other members, for the most part, were tradesmen working in carpentry, bricklaying, blacksmithing, and the like. Some were clearly men of wealth. John Hall, a 34-year-old private of Company C, was the owner of a plough manufacturing concern. His net worth, at the time of his enlistment, was close to $80,000. Richard C. Dale, an individual who would later play a notable role in the regiment, came from a prominent doctor's family.

The unit would spend the next few weeks in Pittsburgh before its ultimate departure for the field. Drills and parades were

Henry F. Eggers
Eighteen-year-old farmer and private in
Company H.

Richard C. Dale
First lieutenant in Company G and son
of a prominent Allegheny doctor.
The Story of the 116th Pennsylvania

a daily occurrence around the streets of Pittsburgh and Allegheny City. Reverend, now Colonel, Clark continued to perform his pastoral functions in his local congregation, as well as his military role. Each Sunday, his church was packed with the men from his regiment, as well as the hordes of well-wishers who prayed for the safe return of their loved ones. James B. Ross, a private in Company G, kept a detailed diary of his days in the 123rd. On August 10, Private Ross attended a service at the colonel's church with "4,000 to 5,000" worshippers present. The *Pittsburgh Gazette* wrote of the service: "Mr. Clark then proceeded to address this immense audience . . . The discourse, which was replete with eloquence, patriotism, and christianity, was listened to with breathless attention and could not be received with the unqualified approbation of every christian and loyal person present . . ."[11]

The men did not spend their entire term of service in the friendly environs of Pittsburgh. On August 20, 1862, the regiment was ordered to Harrisburg for its formal mustering in. Before they left, a large crowd of over five thousand people lined the station to bid the men goodbye. Thomas W. Howe, a prominent leader in Allegheny City, presented each member of Company C with the "Book of Common Prayer." Mr. Howe admonished the men to "[m]ake it your morning and evening habit to look up to him as your surest protector."[12] He concluded his remarks by reaffirming the regiment's humble beginning in Reverend Clark's church and reminded the men to "[c]ultivate and proclaim a living abiding faith in Him, protectant in season and out of season in the discharge of every duty, whether as soldiers of the Union under the glorious stars and stripes, or as soldiers under the still more glorious banner—the banner of the Cross . . ."[13]

Upon their arrival in Harrisburg, the men marched to Camp Curtin, a military camp on the outskirts of Harrisburg, to obtain their "clothes and other articles necessary for a soldier's life."[14] The members of the 123rd were not overly impressed with the new encampment. In an anonymous letter to the *Pittsburgh Gazette*, a member of the 123rd wrote that the camp was the "most filthy place I ever saw."[15] The men were also equally unimpressed

Colonel Clark's Grand Triumphant March

The above song was specifically written for the 123rd by Professor W. T. Wamelink when it was leaving for the field. The *Pittsburgh Post* noted in its October 6, 1862, edition that it was "lively, harmonious and brilliant."

with the quality of arms and clothing that were furnished by the state. Christian Rhein, a corporal in Company B, more than 45 years later still remembered that "we were given the worst and shoddiest clothing and for some arms some Austrian rifles about par with the clothing, so I guess they understood grafting as well as now."[16]

But the inferior quality of the regiment's clothing and arms did not deter the high command from ordering the regiment to Washington. On the very day that the unit arrived in Harrisburg, the men were ordered to board another train for Washington. They initially went through Baltimore and arrived in the capital at approximately 1:00 P.M. on the 22nd of August. Private Matthew H. Borland, a 24-year-old farmer in Company G and another diarist of the regiment's movements, described the unit's entrance into the nation's capital:

> Arrived at the capital about 2:00 P.M., ate at the "Soldiers' Retreat," and started about 5 P.M. for Camp Stanton, Arlington Heights, Va., 6 miles from the Federal City with knapsacks, accouterments and guns . . . all of which tried the boys pretty well. Arrive in camp about 10 P.M., pitched our tents amidst the greatest confusion, laid ourselves down on the ground for the first time and slept soundly until morning.[17]

The regiment remained at Camp Stanton from August 23 to the afternoon of the 27th. During this time, the men began to get their first taste of "soldiering." Guard duty, camp cooking, and discipline took up much of the time at Camp Stanton.

On August 25, the regiment began its first full week in the field. While these new soldiers had clearly come to the realization that life in the field was different, these early days helped to diminish many of their fears about military life. The weather was pleasant and there was a certain tranquility about the camp. But the men soon learned a valuable lesson about military life: everything is subject to abrupt change. On August 27, the regiment learned this lesson well when the placidity of camp life was suddenly shattered.

On that date, the regiment began its day as usual. The companies drilled in the morning and continued their normal camp routines throughout the afternoon. Unbeknownst to the regiment, the entire Army of Northern Virginia was moving north toward Manassas. The Union high command, fearing this northern movement, began to move all available regiments westward to support John Pope's Army of Virginia.

The following day, August 28, the battle of Second Manassas began. At 6 P.M., General Thomas "Stonewall" Jackson attacked an isolated Federal brigade at Brawner's farm. This limited engagement had no clear-cut winner. The next day, Pope became the aggressor and renewed his attack against Jackson's isolated corps. However, Jackson had established a strong defensive position behind an unfinished railroad embankment. Throughout the day, Pope struck Jackson's defensive line in a number of uncoordinated assaults. During the late afternoon, a Federal division captured a portion of Jackson's line, but was unable to hold the position because of a strong counterattack by A. P. Hill's corps.

During this initial phase of the battle, the 123rd was oblivious to the plight of the Union army. But the next day, August 29, the regiment got its first inkling that a battle was developing. Private Borland recorded that the regiment "[r]eceived orders this evening 'Pack knapsacks and be ready to move at a moments warning.'"[18] The order to march did not come until the next day.

On Friday, August 30, after Pope unsuccessfully attacked Jackson's forces, General James Longstreet unexpectedly struck the left flank of Pope's army and caused a general collapse of the Federal position. After a delaying action on Chinn Ridge and Henry Hill, Pope evacuated the entire army across Bull Run and staved off a total disaster. This Federal retreat mobilized the regiments that were in the vicinity of Washington.

At one o'clock on the 30th, the 123rd was ordered in the direction of Fairfax to help form a defensive line for the Federal retreat. This was the first time that either diarist made any statements regarding the battle. Private Borland noted in his diary: "Today there was a battle between Gen. Pope and Stonewall Jackson. Could hear the sound of cannon all day although it was twenty miles distant."[19]

Private
Robert W. Hemphill[†]

MEN
OF THE
123RD PA

Captain
David E. Adams*

Corporal
Frank P. Kohen*

Captain
John S. Bell*

Sergeant
Samuel Taggart[‡]

Private
John Bradley*

* *Under the Maltese Cross*
† USAMHI
‡ *The Story of the 116th Pennsylvania*

On the 31st, the regiment was ordered out on picket duty. The men saw the first evidence of the Federal retreat. Private Borland reported that he saw General McClellan and two of his staff pass along the Leesburg and Washington turnpike. He noted that over ". . .[s]ixty wagons passed this forenoon in one train" and that he and a number of pickets "took four stragglers from Pope's army and sent them to the Col.'s headquarters."[20]

Meanwhile, a number of new developments were taking place which soon involved the 123rd. A dispatch from the Headquarters of the Army of the Potomac mentioned the 123rd by name for the first time. The dispatch noted that the 123rd was to be provisionally brigaded with the 131st, 133rd, and 134th Pennsylvania. The dispatch further stated that the brigade was "now in front of Fort Ward, & c., ha[d] been ordered to report to Col. R. O. Tyler, for duty as part of the garrison works."[21] The

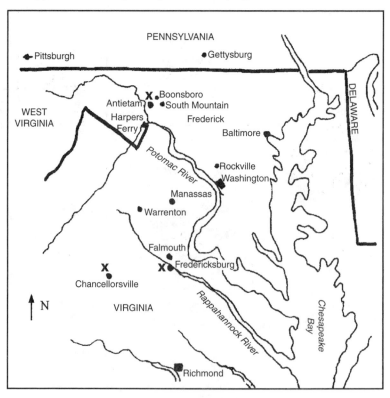

Field of Operations

regiment's provisional commander, in this line, was Brigadier General D. P. Woodbury. Of the 3,923 men that made up the brigade, all but 165 were present for duty.[22]

These were desperate times for the Union and, as such, they required desperate measures. On September 1, amid a torrential downpour, Jackson attacked a column of Pope's army at Chantilly. While Pope escaped into the defenses at Washington, every available regiment was sent to the front to cover the new Confederate threat. The 123rd had only been in Washington for less than two weeks, but was nonetheless rushed to cover the army's retreat. The organizational structure, therefore, had little time to be set. For whatever reason, the four new Pennsylvania regiments were provisionally brigaded together. Colonel Peter Hollingshead Allabach of the 131st became the commander of the brigade.

Colonel Allabach was a 37-year-old resident of Luzerne County, Pennsylvania, at the time of his enlistment in August of 1862. In 1844, he enlisted in the regular army for a term of five years. He was assigned to Company E, Third United States Infantry, and at the start of the Mexican War was ordered to Mexico where he participated in every battle of the war, except the battle for Buena Vista. As a result of his conduct, he was promoted to sergeant after his first six months of service. Colonel Allabach served his five-year term and was mustered out of the regular army on November 25, 1849.[23] In May of 1852, he was appointed by Governor William Bigler of Pennsylvania as a brigadier general of the Uniformed Militia of Luzerne

Peter Hollingshead Allabach
Colonel of the 131st Pennsylvania and a veteran of the Mexican War. He would be the commander of the brigade for the 123rd's entire term.
Lang Collection

County. On August 16, 1862, he was commissioned by Governor Curtin as colonel of the 131st.

Colonel Clark was not totally pleased with the selection of Colonel Allabach as the commander of the brigade. Since Colonel Clark's regiment was mustered in first, he felt that he, not Colonel Allabach, was the senior colonel and, as such, should have been appointed the brigade commander. In a letter to the *Gazette* on October 8, 1862, he explained that Colonel Allabach only received command "through personal and political favoritism." While the commander of the 123rd thanked "a kind Providence for relieving [him] from the duties of th[is] position," he could not help but write that "[a]ll I ask, [on] behalf of myself and men is simple justice."[24]

While Colonel Clark may have felt the selection of Colonel Allabach was politically motivated, there is little doubt that his selection was the better choice. Colonel Allabach clearly had a more extensive military background and was better suited to command a group of raw recruits, although the men were not totally enamored with the colonel. A captain of the 155th, a regiment that later became part of the brigade in the middle of September, made the following observation regarding Colonel Allabach:

> Although obedience is the first duty of a soldier, that does not hinder him from having his likes or dislikes. He soon learns whether an officer is doing all he can to lighten his burdens, and is trying to make him comfortable, or whether he tries to show his authority by adding unnecessary duties to make his life more miserable . . . [O]ur Brigade Commander, Col. Allabach, belongs to the latter. The title he usually receives when he is referred to is "Old Allabach" or some other disrespectful term.[25]

Except for the letter from Colonel Clark, no record can be found of the 123rd's opinion of Colonel Allabach. In any event, regardless of the feelings of these officers and soldiers, Colonel Allabach remained the brigade commander during the 123rd's entire term.

The next eleven days, September 1 through September 12, were filled with regimental drills, picket duty, and the mundane task of digging trenches. During this period of time, the regiment encamped near Fairfax Seminary and was assigned to the V Corps. The brigade, which still consisted of the 123rd, 131st, 133rd, and the 134th, was provisionally assigned to Brigadier General William D. Whipple's divisional command. Whipple's brigade, along with two other brigades, were ordered "to hold the rifle-pits and defend the works from Fort Craig through Forts Ward, Worth, &c., to Fort Ellsworth." The dispatch further stated that "Allabach's brigade will . . . be posted and held ready to push out on the Leesburg or Little River turnpike. Allabach will picket on the Little River pike and railroad, having the main guard at the crossing of Cameron and Holmes Run."[26]

Throughout this period, the regiment continued to see the tattered remains of the Army of Virginia. Private Borland wrote on September 3 that he saw "W. J. Rippey coming across the road, bare footed and looking rather badly used up." On September 5, he described an older regiment and noted that they "had been through the campaigns of the Peninsula; it drilled beautifully but was not but a skeleton—not more than three hundred men."[27]

This short interlude allowed the men some time to reflect on their first month in the army, as well as to contemplate the many fears that lay ahead. Private Borland described his first month in rather positive terms: "[I]t has been rather an eventful month in my life . . . I have saw much which if rightly used will be beneficial to me through (life)."[28] Private Robert Hemphill, however, was not as upbeat as his comrade: "I would advise Samuel to stay at home as long as he can for if he gets here once he will be likely to wish he was home. You need not tell this to anybody out of the family but there is no disguising the fact that soldiering is something more than mere fun."[29] The men's fears revolved around the increasing reports that the Confederate army had moved north. Many feared for the safety of their loved ones back home. Private Hemphill summed up the feelings of the regiment when he observed that the men would rather "[be] sen[t] . . . back to Pittsburgh to fight" since "we could do it with a better will there than here . . ."[30]

But the commander of the regiment still had concerns about the fitness of his men for battle. There were valid reasons for Colonel Clark's concerns. Very few of the officers of the 123rd had any military experience. Further, the first few weeks of the regiment's time in the field had been spent moving from place to place to counter the anticipated threats of the enemy. As a result, very little quality time had been spent training the men in the art of warfare. It was with much trepidation that Colonel Clark mentioned that "[t]he men need constant attention, that they may be ready for the battle field. All officers, I regret to say, don't realize their responsibility. They don't feel that they are accountable for the lives of their men to a large degree."[31]

On September 12, Colonel Clark was ordered to put the regiment in motion. Training would have to wait. The regiment spent the early morning of the 13th sleeping on the pavement in Washington. At sunrise, the unit was ordered to leave their knapsacks and all other superfluous items behind. It was the recommendation of the officers that each member only take his "blanket and overcoat."[32] However, the evidence seems to clearly indicate that many members of this regiment, as well as other regiments, did not heed the warnings of their officers.

After their knapsacks were stowed, the regiment marched to the arsenal to exchange their rifles. The regiment was also granted a special treat during its brief stay in Washington. The men in the regiment, eager to see the president, ran out into the road to see Lincoln ride a horse down the road. That evening, the men again observed the president riding in a carriage under the escort of his cavalry.

During this short stop, the final organization of the division was established. On September 12, 1862, Brigadier General Andrew Atkinson Humphreys was offered command of the Third Division, V Corps. This division consisted of Allabach's brigade and the brigade commanded by Brigadier General Erastus B. Tyler. Upon the organization of the division, there was a slight realignment in Allabach's brigade. The 134th Pennsylvania, which up until that time had been a member of this brigade, was transferred to Tyler's brigade. In its place, the 155th Pennsylvania, a three-year regiment that had been recruited in Pittsburgh at the same time as the 123rd, was added. As a result, Tyler's brigade consisted of the 91st, 126th, 129th, and the 134th Pennsylvania.[33] Allabach's brigade contained the 123rd, 131st, 133rd, and the 155th.[34] Tyler's brigade was designated as the 1st Brigade and Allabach's the 2nd.

All of the regiments, except the 91st, were new regiments. The 91st was mustered into service in December of 1861, for three years, but up until this time had only performed provost duties in and around Washington.[35] The 123rd, 126th, 129th, 131st, 133rd, and 134th were all newly mustered nine-month regiments. The 155th, although a three-year regiment, only entered military service in August of 1862.

General Andrew A. Humphreys, the new division commander, was born on November 2, 1810, in Philadelphia, Pennsylvania. In 1827, at the age of 16, Humphreys was appointed to West Point where he graduated in 1831 in the upper half of his class and received an assignment to the artillery. He served in the Seminole War in Florida during 1836. In 1838, he received an appointment to the Corps of Topographical Engineers, where he remained until the beginning of the Civil War. During these years, he undertook various surveys for the government and, by all accounts, was very accomplished in his field. At the outbreak of

Andrew Atkinson Humphreys
Brigadier general and division commander. The division consisting of the 123rd was his first field command. He would go on to have a distinguished record for the remainder of the war.
USAMHI (MOLLUS)

the war, Humphreys was in ill health, which prevented his early entrance into field command. On December 1, 1861, he was assigned to General McClellan as a special assistant where his duties entailed preparing maps of the intended fields of operation. On March 5, 1862, prior to the Peninsula Campaign, he was appointed as an additional aide-de-camp to General McClellan, with the rank of colonel, and formally given the title Chief of Topographical Engineers, Army of the Potomac. On April 28, 1862, he was appointed to Brigadier General of Volunteers.[36]

After performing admirably during the Peninsula Campaign, General Humphreys addressed a letter to the secretary of war that requested he be relieved from his duties in the Topographical Corps and assigned a field command. The request was finally granted on August 23, 1862, when General Humphreys was directed to report to Brigadier General Silas Casey in Washington. After a brief visit with his family in Pennsylvania, Humphreys arrived in Washington on August 30, 1862. He reported to General Casey, who was in dire need of field commanders.[37] Since Tyler's and Allabach's brigades had already been sent to Washington for deployment, a divisional commander was needed. This critical need for commanders helps to explain why General Humphreys, with little or no field experience, was assigned a new division of untrained recruits.

The appointment to command the newly formed division was hardly a choice assignment. The men in the division were poorly equipped and in desperate need of supplies. Over nine hundred of the Austrian rifles in Allabach's brigade were unserviceable, and a requisition for more serviceable arms had been rejected by the Ordnance Department. Further, Allabach's men were without sufficient rations to sustain a long forced march. Each man had only two days of rations in his haversack and the brigade had not been in the field long enough to collect cattle for future needs.[38] One can only wonder, after Humphreys became aware of these deficiencies, whether he questioned his request for field command. The brigades were hardly prepared for combat.

As if the condition of his brigades were not bad enough, the situation continued to grow steadily worse. For some reason, General Henry W. Halleck, the General in Chief of the Army, perceived that General Humphreys had refused to take command of his division. Because of this, he issued a dispatch which stated: "Headquarters of the Army, Washington, September 13, 1862. Unless General Humphreys immediately leaves to take command of his division in the field, he will be arrested for disobedience of orders."[39] Nothing could have been further from the truth.

General Humphreys was presented with an almost impossible task. He was ordered to lead a group of raw troops on a forced march in less than 24 hours. The fact that General Humphreys had the division formed and marching by September 14 should have been an occasion for praise, not criticism. But General Halleck did not see it that way, and his insinuations clearly upset General Humphreys. In March of 1863, after a belief that he had been denied promotion because of this incident, Humphreys requested a Court of Inquiry in order to clear his name. In the letter requesting the hearing, the general provided a detailed statement about the events of September 12 and 13. He reiterated that Allabach's entire brigade had not reached Washington until daybreak of the 13th. Humphreys explained that upon speaking to Allabach, he learned that his brigade had been marching from one fort to another when the order to report to Washington had been received. As such, close to "one-half to two thirds" of the brigade's "provisions, ammunition and forage" had been left at the old camp.[40]

Further, the general also informed Secretary Edwin M. Stanton that he had to deal with the brigade's "utterly unserviceable" rifles. Upon speaking with Colonel Allabach in Washington, Humphreys was informed that nine hundred guns in the brigade had "hammers or nipples broken" and that more "were breaking every day." Those men who had serviceable rifles had no more than 60 rounds of ammunition because the ammunition wagons had been left at the previous camp. With all of these problems in mind, General Humphreys felt that it was necessary to postpone the September 13th march.[41]

There is no evidence of any official action having been taken on Humphreys' request. On July 12, 1863, General Humphreys was promoted to major general, which indicates that the incident appears not to have tarnished his career. Nevertheless, in following years, General Humphreys was known to bristle when asked about the September 12 dispatch.

The men's initial opinion of General Humphreys was a bit unclear. He was a West Point man who, at the beginning of his command, appeared to be "austere, and disposed to be tyrannical."[42] One subordinate described him as "exacting and precise, an unfeeling bow-legged tyrant."[43] However, as time went on, the men realized that he clearly had their best interests in mind and that he "knew how to command."[44]

The general's personality initially caused some problems in this totally civilian unit. He was known to be polite, but when angered, profanity flowed from his mouth with ease. Charles Anderson Dana, the assistant secretary of war, thought him "one of the loudest swearers" he had known, a man of "distinguished and brilliant profanity."[45] He was a man not known for his patience, and when he first assumed command, "[h]e knew little of human nature in civilians" and by some accounts "was not well fitted to handle citizen volunteers."[46] In any event, by the time the division was mustered out, the men almost unanimously agreed that General Humphreys transformed the group into an effective fighting unit.

On Sunday, September 14, Colonel Clark's regiment of "Christian patriots" left the safety of Washington accompanied by the rest of Humphreys' Division. Private Ross wrote in his diary that the regiment began marching at five o'clock and traveled 18 miles on the Rockville Road. The march was not good for all of the members of the regiment. He later wrote that "[o]n the march there was one of the wagons of our train upset into the creek hurting several pretty badly."[47] Unfortunately, one of the injured, James Doudgeon, became the first casualty of the regiment.

Throughout the day on the 14th, the cannonading which opened the Battle of South Mountain could be heard in the distance. General Humphreys, aware that the cannon fire might have a negative effect on the men, spent the entire day riding with the division. Members of the 155th remembered that "General Humphreys . . . made his appearance at the head of the Division during the day, and became very conspicuous, riding backward and forward along the column on his superb charger, appearing to be the very embodiment of energy and martial bearing."[48] After a long, but productive first day's march, General Humphreys and the division camped near Rockville, Maryland, at the very site of General McClellan's headquarters two days earlier. The men went to sleep in an open field and slept soundly under the stars.

On September 15, the regiment awakened early and resumed its march northward beginning at 5 A.M. The unit marched for approximately 12 hours; stopping at 5 P.M. and bivouacking in an orchard in the vicinity of Clarksburg, Maryland. Private Borland noted that the regiment "[m]arched today about 15 miles; the boys were all a good deal fatigued; the country was rather poor and covered with pine forests but looked more like home than VA. being fenced and inhabited."[49]

On September 16, the regiment was again awakened at an early hour, 3 A.M., to continue the march. The regiment began the trek on the extreme left of the brigade and passed through the towns of Clarksburg, Hyattstown, and Urbana. At the end of the day's march, the regiment bivouacked near Frederick, Maryland, on the banks of the Monocacy River. Private Borland described the area as being "very well improved" and the "land evidently of . . . good quality" with the principal crops being corn and tobacco. This "well improved" land had not escaped the destructive aspects of war. Near the regiment's camp on the Monocacy, the men saw the remains of "a demolished bridge and R. Road bridge."[50] Other members from the brigade also noticed the devastating effects of war. Private Ross wrote of seeing "two dead rebels buried alongside the creek."[51] A member of the 155th remembered "a dead man entirely naked, lying by a tree."[52] Another member of the 155th recalled "the corpse of a negro killed in the blowing up of the bridge."[53]

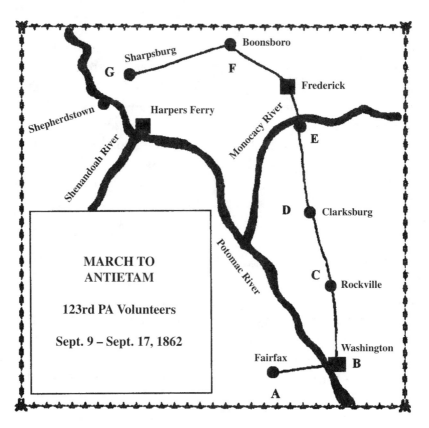

MARCH TO
ANTIETAM

123rd PA Volunteers

Sept. 9 – Sept. 17, 1862

A. Camp established on September 9 in Fairfax between Fairfax Seminary and Leising Pike.

B. Ordered to Washington on September 12, arriving on the morning of September 13.

C. Left Washington in the morning of September 14. Marched all day and camped for the night in Rockville, Maryland.

D. Resumed march in the morning of the 15th and marched all day and late into the night. Camped near Clarksburg, Maryland.

E. Commenced march early on the 16th and arrived in Frederick in the evening.

F. Remained in Frederick until 4 P.M. to protect the city from attack. Set out for Sharpsburg at 4 P.M.

G. Marched all night on the 17th and arrived at the battlefield in the morning or early afternoon on the 18th. Formed around the Pry House and relieved Morrell's Division.

The march was more strenuous than all the prior days'. The weather was hot and the roads were dusty. Many of the knapsacks, overcoats, and impediments that were not left in Washington were now discarded. The heat posed a serious problem for the regiment. Many of the men lagged "far behind the advance of the Regiment unable to maintain the speed." General Humphreys and Colonel Allabach, "riding superb horses," urged these men on, but night overtook many of them, and they were forced to "turn in at [the] points where they broke down."[54] It began raining late at night, but the men never noticed.

Upon its arrival at Frederick, the division received orders from General Fitz John Porter to guard the town. In a letter General Humphreys wrote to Secretary of War Edwin M. Stanton on April 3, 1863, he explained that upon arrival, he "received orders from General Porter to take a position in front of the town, to cover it" and to watch his left.[55] The next day, after carefully examining the approaches to the town, the general established a number of advanced outposts to protect the roads leading into town. He also made arrangements with the local telegraph office to send any intelligence that was received from the vicinity of Harpers Ferry. Clearly, the Union commanders were still unclear of General Jackson's intentions, who was known to be in this area.

As a result of the September 16 orders, the division remained in Frederick for the majority of the daylight hours of September 17, 1862. The great battle at Antietam Creek began and ended that day, but the regiment arrived on the field too late to be engaged in the fight. During this momentary reprieve, the men used the Monocacy River for a much-needed bath.

During this short rest, the regiment witnessed a rather disheartening scene that was precipitated by General Stonewall Jackson's capture of the Union garrison at Harpers Ferry. The victory by General Jackson netted over 15,000 prisoners who were on their way to Washington to await parole. The men sadly observed these soldiers passing by. One member of the brigade wrote that the prisoners "appeared sad, and many . . . betrayed despondency as they spoke of the great prowess of Stonewall Jackson."

This same individual could not help but feel that the "incident was certainly one which tended to chill the ardor of the most enthusiastic patriot."[56]

The regiment did not have a great amount of time to contemplate the fate of those who were captured at Harpers Ferry. At 2:30 P.M., General Humphreys received orders from General Fitz John Porter that his division was to hurry to the field.[57] After leaving Frederick, the regiment took the National Road and followed it to Middletown where the men turned onto the road to Boonsboro. Upon the regiment's arrival in Boonsboro, the streets were filled with wounded soldiers being conveyed to the rear. Every available building in the city had been appropriated as a hospital for the wounded and dying. The cries of these men filled the air as the men of the 123rd continued their trek. Many could not help but wonder what fate lay ahead.

The regiment witnessed the passing of the body of Colonel James H. Childs, a native of Pittsburgh and commander of the 4th Pennsylvania Cavalry, who had been killed the previous day. Many members of the regiment had personally known Colonel Childs or had attended his many recruiting presentations in the city. Colonel Edward J. Allen, the commander of the 155th, stated: "We could realize what his death meant to those at home — a sorrow, as we were to know, but one of many thousands, because of the dead whose bodies as yet lay stark upon the bloody field of Antietam."[58]

After arriving on the field, the 123rd formed its battle line around the Pry House, which had served as the headquarters for General McClellan. The general had since vacated the area, so the men did not have the opportunity to see the commander but could see the remnants of the prior day's battle. The exact time of the regiment's arrival at the Pry House is not known, but according to all available data, the men reached there between 11:00 A.M. and 3:00 P.M.

Corporal Christian Rhein recalled that at the regiment's arrival "our Colonel John B. Clark ha[d] us drawn up in line and addressed us telling us in particular to aim for the belt."[59] Private

Ross' recollection of the first moments after the regiment's arrival was a little different. He wrote in his diary:

> The Col. mounted his horse and was at our head. He said: "Gentleman of the 123d, you have been brought here to the full of the enemy, it is possible that you might go into active service today. Keep cool, have good courage and have but one object in view and let that be rebels. When you shoot, shoot that they may die. Hold our line of battle with all your might."[60]

But the battle was not renewed that day. The armies held their positions during the day; after dark, General Robert E. Lee and the Army of Northern Virginia recrossed the Potomac and returned to Virginia.

On September 19, the regiment received orders at 10 A.M. to move forward about one mile and form a line of battle on the ground that was previously held by the enemy. The regiment quickly moved to the location, but secured orders late in the afternoon to pursue the enemy as it retreated across the Potomac.

On September 20, the 123rd moved forward in line of battle along the banks of the Potomac, opposite Shepherdstown, Virginia (now West Virginia). The members of the regiment witnessed the artillery shelling the Confederates on the opposite side of the river. This was the last engagement the regiment witnessed for some time, as the plight of the 123rd, for the next six weeks, was picket duty and drill at Camp McAuley. The camp consisted of a tract of land located in the suburbs of Sharpsburg, on the banks of the Potomac. The exact location can not be accurately pinpointed, but in all likelihood, it was located near the Grove Farm.

Although the regiment was within 60 miles of Washington, their urgent appeals for shelter tents and supplies went unheeded by the governmental bureaucrats. In order to protect themselves from the weather, the men were forced to build impromptu shelters from any material that they could find. Private Hemphill wrote in a letter to his father that "[w]e have to sleep under sheds that we built out of boards as our tents were left behind . . . when we started on the last march."[61] The exposure to the elements had a devastating effect on the health of the regiment, which was addressed by Colonel Clark on two different occasions. In a letter dated September 24 he noted: "This leaves us camped on the banks of the Potomac. The location is more favorable for catching ague than anything else. The ground is part of the late battlefield, and is covered with graves, wounded men and substances calculated to make the atmosphere injurious to health." On October 5, the colonel wrote that "[I]t is [a] wonder . . . to me that there is not more sickness among us. There is so much carelessness in casting tainted beef out to rot all over the brigade camp, and so many things are left strewed promiscuously over the ground that I cannot wonder at our general health."[62]

Grave of John Marshall

In the days following the battle, graves of slain soldiers were everywhere. The men of the 123rd observed many in their movements around Sharpsburg. One such grave, memorialized by the famous picture by Alexander Gardner, shows the temporary resting place of Private John Marshall of the 28th Pennsylvania Infantry. Private Marshall was a resident of Allegheny City, and a member of Colonel Clark's church.

The colonel's worst fears unfortunately came to fruition. Not all the losses, however, were due to death. In October, three members of the regiment were discharged on surgeon's certificates of disability. Company A lost two of its members: Private Henry C. Campbell on October 1 and Corporal David A. Bennett on October 8. Company B lost one: Sergeant John Vandevender on October 29. In the two months since the regiment left Pittsburgh, five men in the regiment had died of disease or accident, three had been discharged on surgeon's certificates, and nine had deserted.

The 123rd was not the only regiment faced with this dilemma. The 155th also confronted a similar predicament. The *Gazette* painted a rather dismal portrait of this regiment in an article published on October 17, 1862:

> We regret to learn that Col. Allen's fine regiment (155th) is suffering very much from want of medicine. Strange as it may appear, the government has not yet provided them with drugs, as indispensable to the men while becoming "acclimated." As a consequence, there are now 200 on the sick list—most of them suffering from trifling ailments, to be sure, but sufficient to disqualify from duty.[63]

Unfortunately for the 155th, like the 123rd, the much-needed supplies arrived too late. Twelve members of the unit died of disease in the weeks before the division left Sharpsburg, or a short time thereafter.

The weeks in Sharpsburg, while trying, did provide the men with some much-needed rest and money, their much-anticipated regimental colors, spiritual ministrations by their commander, and a visit from their commander in chief. All of these events, while somewhat minor in the overall scheme of things, helped to prepare the regiment for the upcoming campaign.

Most of this time was spent along the Potomac River, across from Shepherdstown, Virginia. Except for a number of cold and rainy evenings, these periods were pleasantly spent. Private Borland scribbled in his diary on October 7: "We stood on duty four hours viz, from two to six A.M., there were no alarms—'all was quiet along the Potomac'; a most beautiful night it was, fair Cynthia flaming with resplendent beauty, casting fantastic shaped shadows from the rugged rocks which from the bank of the canal; the boys enjoyed themselves hugely, washing, fishing, and letter writing forming the principal amusements . . ."[64]

On October 5, the men collected their first military pay. Each soldier received 27 dollars: 25 dollars as their first installment of the Federal bounty, and 2 dollars for their enlistment fee. Although most men shipped the money home to their families, others used some or all of it to purchase food and clothing from the camp sutler. The camp sutler permitted the men to buy on credit, taking as collateral their monthly pay. Private Hemphill described the process: "We got checks on our sutler for whatever we wanted to get. I drew three dollars. It is about done but I can get more if I want it. It will be deducted from our pay on the first pay day."[65]

The regiment also finally received its state colors during its stay in Sharpsburg. Flag presentations usually took place at Harrisburg, upon a regiment's mustering into state service. In the case of the 123rd, however, the presentation was delayed because the regiment was needed in the field. As a result, the formal presentation of the state flag did not occur until October 15, 1862. Seven of the other regiments in the brigade, all new Pennsylvania regiments, also received their colors that day. Assistant Adjutant General Williams, on behalf of Governor Curtin, presented the state flag to Colonel Clark. Governor Curtin had originally been scheduled to present the colors, but had been otherwise detained and could not make the trip. Both Privates Borland and Ross attended the presentation. Private Borland wrote that "[t]he regiments of our brigade were presented with the State flags by assistant Adj. Gen. Williams as the representative of Gov. Curtin; he made a speech to the field officers representing the regiments and the Col. replied for the regiments after the presentation of their respective colors. Our Col. 'took the rag off the bush' in replying and we gave him three rousing cheers."[66] Sergeant James Caldwell of K received the honor of carrying the flag for the remainder of the regiment's term.

The colonel found time, during his stay, to administer to the spiritual needs of the wounded. Many of the injured were Confederate soldiers. The colonel could not help but wonder how his parishioners at home would view his ministries. He attempted to justify his actions "as a Christian act to those who are suffering." But he also wrote that "[s]ome of them appeared gratified, others looked amazed, and others appeared insensible to all the claims of God upon them."[67] There is no evidence that any member of his parish or the community ever registered a complaint against Colonel Clark for his ministrations to the Confederate wounded.

But by far the most memorable event while in Sharpsburg was the review of the regiment by President Lincoln. This event took place on October 3 and was eagerly anticipated by all. While most grumbled on the day of the event, due to poor planning, the lasting memory of their introduction to the president undoubtedly remained with them for years to come. Private Ross described the review as a "grand affair" with a "salute of 22 guns"and the "cheers of thousands."[68] Colonel Clark was not as enthusiastic when he wrote home on October 5: ". . . [Y]esterday, Father Abraham, from Washington, and Gen. McClellan reviewed about 30,000 troops in this vicinity. I could not say that it was either grand or comfortable. Our division was drawn out in line at 9 A.M., and it was 2 P.M. when these high officials made their appearance . . . Our brigade and some others had the pleasure of standing on a ploughed field all this time. Many of the boys felt more pain than pleasure. It reminded me of great expectations followed by small gratification."[69]

Colonel Clark also described the general appearance of the president on this momentous occasion. He told his parishioners that he appeared "care worn" and seemed oppressed by the heat of the day. Joshua Chamberlain, the hero of Little Round Top and second in command of the 20th Maine, was equally struck by his tired mien: "There were deep lines in his bearded face, there were

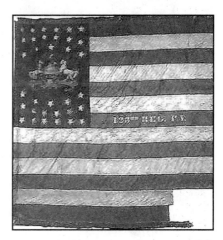

Regimental Flag

The 123rd's state colors were presented on October 5, 1862, somewhere in the vicinity of Sharpsburg.

Pennsylvania Capitol Preservation Committee

shadow's around the President's eyes. He looked as though he was carrying the burdens of the entire country."[70] Another member of the army was far less complimentary: "Oh! he is homely beyond all description. There may be great executive power there also, but he looks like a very inferior centre piece for this Republic."

But the burdens of this president, and the men of the 123rd, were only beginning. The defining moment for the Christian patriots was fast approaching. The regiment had thus far endured the rigors of a forced march and the monotony of a Civil War encampment. They were now moving toward their first encounter with the enemy. At the end of October, the men began their trek to Fredericksburg and in the process, their rendezvous with destiny.

Lincoln Visits Antietam

Above: This photo was taken on October 3, 1862, and shows President Lincoln, General McClellan, General Humphreys *(second from the right)* and a number of other Union generals just after they completed their review of the V Corps. This picture was widely reproduced by Gardner and undoubtedly purchased by many members of the regiment as a memento of Lincoln's visit to their camp. *Left:* Close-up of General Humphreys. To his right is then-Captain George Armstrong Custer.

Library of Congress

Chapter Two
March to Fredericksburg

Lead on O King eternal. The day of march has come . . .

After nearly three months in the army, the men of the 123rd had yet to actively participate in a battle. They were eager to prove their mettle in combat, but were beginning to feel that they may never face the enemy. This failure to see any form of action clearly caused some frustration among the men in the regiment. Their commander in chief also felt the same frustration as his soldiers. At the October review of the troops, the president spoke with General McClellan about his plans for the future. No concrete answers were given by the general. In the days and weeks that followed this meeting, Lincoln continually prodded his commander to submit a comprehensive plan for the pursuit of the enemy.

In the latter part of October, Lincoln ordered McClellan to move against Lee. On October 26, McClellan wired Lincoln and indicated that the army could not presently move due to "fatigued" and "sore tongued" horses. The president wired back in utter frustration: "Will you pardon me for asking what the horses of your army have done since the battle of Antietam that fatigues anything?"[1] The next day, whether out of fear or lack of further excuses, McClellan directed the IX Corps to cross the Potomac and move south.

The 123rd was oblivious to these new developments. Both Privates Ross and Borland only mentioned the disagreeable weather in their diaries from October 26 to October 29. But on October 30, 1862, this relative calm changed as the regiment received orders from General Humphreys to strike tents and prepare to march. To most, this was their first experience in breaking

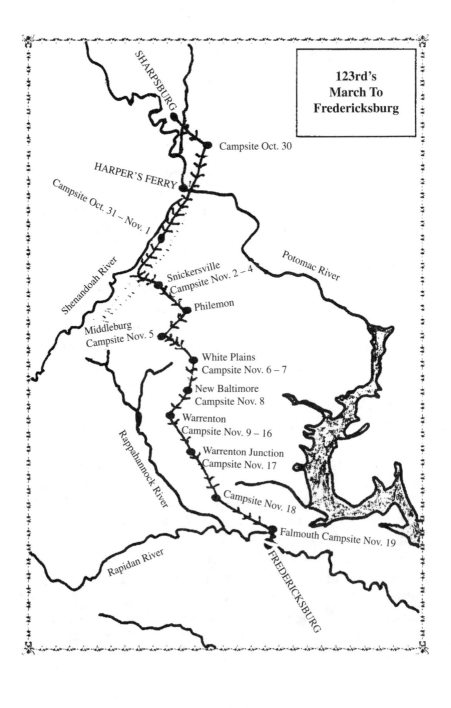

SHARPSBURG

Campsite Oct. 30

HARPER'S FERRY

Campsite Oct. 31 – Nov. 1

123rd's
March To
Fredericksburg

Shenandoah River

Potomac River

Snickersville
Campsite Nov. 2 – 4

Philemon

Middleburg
Campsite Nov. 5

White Plains
Campsite Nov. 6 – 7

New Baltimore
Campsite Nov. 8

Warrenton
Campsite Nov. 9 – 16

Rappahannock River

Warrenton Junction
Campsite Nov. 17

Campsite Nov. 18

Falmouth Campsite Nov. 19

Rapidan River

FREDERICKSBURG

camp. One soldier could not help but comment that the entire process seemed a "good deal like leaving home."[2]

At 2 P.M. the brigade received orders to form on the parade ground. The men of the 123rd were the first to answer the call.[3] The division was aligned for the march, with General Tyler's brigade taking the lead, followed by the division's artillery.[4] Allabach's brigade brought up the rear with Companies B and G detailed as the rear guard.[5]

At 3 P.M., the order was given to march. The route the division initially followed took the men through the streets of Sharpsburg and across the Antietam battlefield. The troops crossed Antietam Creek over what is known as Burnside's Bridge and turned right onto the Mountain Road. Many had trouble keeping up on the steep road. At dark, the group reached the top of South Mountain and began their downhill trek. The march down seemed more difficult and the weary soldiers "fell out . . . by scores."[6] But their increasing fatigue did not halt the march. All who were able continued long into the night, finally coming to rest at midnight.[7]

Early the next morning, the brigade was again on the move. This march began before dawn and continued for the entire day. At approximately 2 P.M., the regiment reached Harpers Ferry and crossed the Shenandoah River on pontoon bridges. The next day, November 1, the regiment stayed in camp. The only excitement of the day was the mustering in for pay. On November 2, the men awoke at 4:30 A.M. and left camp at 6 A.M., covering between 18 and 20 miles, and finally coming to rest near Snickersville.[8] The next two days, the men remained at this location, with most of the time being spent resting from the rigors of the prior days' marching.

On November 5, the regiment continued their southernly journey. At 10 A.M. the men took the Snickersville and Alexandria turnpike and marched about six miles through a little village called Philemon. They encamped for the night, about three miles from the turnpike, in the town of Middleburg.

The next day, the march began at 6 A.M. and took the regiment through the town of White Plains, a town "situated on the

R.road which leads to Washington via Manassas." The weather, during this portion of the march, became increasingly colder. On November 7, the regiment stayed in camp at White Plains. Private Borland reported that the weather was cold and blustery.[9] Private Ross wrote that there was considerable snow on the ground, "1 to 2 inches deep."[10]

The march continued on the morning of the 8th and proceeded south across the mountains. Private Borland noted that "[a]t North Gap we passed through some beautiful country, almost entirely fenced with stone, the labor of the poor slave; almost every house has its compliments of slave quarters."[11] The quarters were described as "small one story buildings, dirty [and] dingy, . . . built to the rear and a little way off from the mansion." The slaves welcomed the regiment with broad smiles and "crowded along the fences" to greet their liberators. For many of the men, this brief encounter with the institution of slavery helped strengthen their resolve for a Northern victory. As a member of the brigade later wrote: "I think this war will give freedom to the slaves, hope and pray it may."[12]

That evening, the regiment came to rest close to the town of New Baltimore. The next morning at 10 A.M., the regiment again struck their tents. This trek, however, was short and only covered five miles. The regiment halted about one mile outside of Warrenton.

The constant marching and cold weather was beginning to take its toll on the regiment. Men became sick from lack of rest and exposure to the elements. During this period, another member of the regiment died. Private Hemphill, who was fortunate enough to have been assigned to the ambulance corps, wrote to his father about the rigors of the march and the death of his comrade:

> We have come a good distance . . . but I can't say exactly how far. I have got a very good place. I am in the ambulance corps . . . I get all my baggage hauled on a march. The loads the men carry is what makes so many of them sick, I believe. If you would see how many drop behind on a march you

would be surprised. I have pitied some of them much. Some are little boys almost and not able to go any distance till they give out. I hope this war may soon end for it has caused an awful amount of suffering. There was a man out of Co. F of our regt. died the other day while we were on the march. He was in the ambulance when he died. He was the son of McWilliams the horse doctor.[13]

The individual Private Hemphill eluded to was Warren McWilliams, a private in Company F. He is listed in military reports as having died on November 6, 1862. His body was moved from its temporary grave in White Plains to Arlington National Cemetery. Interestingly enough, Private McWilliams is the only member of the 123rd who was granted this honor. He was the tenth member of the regiment to die since its departure from Allegheny City on August 20, 1862.

The regiment had now been on the move for 10 days. In these 10 days, certain events had transpired that precipitated significant changes in the regimental command, and even greater changes in the command of the Army of the Potomac. The change in regimental command came about because of a continual problem that the commanders faced during the march—incessant straggling and foraging in enemy territory. Since this was still during the early stages of the war, the Union hierarchy espoused a certain civility toward noncombatants. Sherman and Grant's theory of all-out-war had not yet been adopted by the president. As such, at the beginning of the march, McClellan had issued strict orders that all property of the enemy was not to be seized or molested. The order further reiterated that "the business of the Union soldier was not to molest, but to protect the peaceful non-combatant citizens,"[14] and that any individual violating this policy would be severely disciplined. However, the soldiers did not heed their commanders' orders. On the second day of the march, General Porter and General Humphreys issued an order stating that the unit commanders would be held personally responsible and liable to court-martial if their men did not pay heed to their prior orders.

All of the threats and orders had little effect on the men of the 123rd. Private Borland was out foraging on November 3, three days after the orders were read, and enacted the confiscation act by appropriating a portion of mutton. Others took chickens, ducks, turkeys, and calves, the only question being "Is the thing fit to eat?"[15] The men were well fed for the first time since they came to the army.

It is not clear how strictly Colonel Clark enforced these orders, but it is known that he was not a true advocate of the policy. While encamped in Sharpsburg, Colonel Clark wrote a letter dated October 5 and made the following observation:

> [I]t is ordered that any soldier found touching property of any kind shall be severely punished . . . I am credibly informed that most of the property through this region is owned by men either in the rebel army or strongly in sympathy with the infamous rebellion; and unless more light gleams upon my darkened mind than I enjoy, I cannot see the justice of the recent order.[16]

How many members of the 123rd became victims of this order is questionable. It is known that the situation became so serious that a group of United States Regulars were detailed as provost guards to capture foragers and stragglers. The regulars were delighted with their new duties. As many as two hundred members of one regiment were arrested on a single day. These men were confined "at the end of the day's march" and "corralled as prisoners in what was called a 'bull-pen,'" where they remained under arrest until morning, when they were discharged.[17]

The enlisted men were not the only individuals expected to obey these orders. Regimental officers were also required to avoid any improper appropriation of civilian property. It is probably safe to say that officers were held to a higher standard than their noncommissioned counterparts. Any violation of these orders by an officer was clearly a more serious situation. Such was the unfortunate fate of Lieutenant Colonel Frederick Gast. His situation was compounded all the more by the fact that his enforcer was none other than General Humphreys himself. Colonel Gast explained the "misunderstanding" in a letter to the editors of the *Gazette*:

> On the march from Sharpsburg, while we were encamped at Snicker's Gap, a young man in the regiment secured and gave me a black mare, belonging to a paroled rebel. I used the animal one day. The second day I was notified to give up the animal to the Division Quarter Master. So soon as we came to a halt for the night, I went in search of said Quarter Master with the full intent of giving up the animal, but unfortunately for me Capt. Morris could not be found, being absent, as I was informed, getting a good supper at a farm house. The next day I delivered up the animal as soon as we reached White Plains. But Gen. Humphreys ordered me under arrest. My case was tried before a court martial, Nov. 15th, while in camp near Warrenton.[18]

The decision in his case was delayed until December 11, 1862, when Lieutenant Colonel Gast was dishonorably discharged and severed from any further authority with the 123rd. Even though all of the captains of the regiment wrote a letter expressing their confidence in him and excusing his conduct on the belief that he did not "deliberately or intentionally appropriate the property of a loyal citizen of the United States,"[19] Colonel Gast still lost his commission. He appealed to Governor Curtin to be recommissioned, but a new lieutenant colonel had already been selected. After his December 11 dismissal, he was never again associated with the 123rd.

During this same period, an ever-escalating game was being played by General McClellan and President Lincoln, which would ultimately lead to a change in the overall command of the army. Following General Lee's retreat from Antietam, the Confederate commander had concentrated his forces in the area of Winchester. Lincoln saw this as a chance for victory since the Army of the Potomac was closer to Richmond than Lee's army. Lincoln knew that in order to seize this opportunity, the army had to move quickly. If McClellan could seize the Orange and Alexandria

Railroad and open a southward route, then he would remain at the head of the army. If he lost the march, then he was to be relieved from command.

By November 3, the outcome had been decided. It had taken McClellan nine days to get his army across the Potomac and concentrated in Warrenton. In the meantime, General James Longstreet, with half of the Army of Virginia, had marched to Culpeper and blocked McClellan's path south. This unexpected move by Longstreet foiled the president's plans; McClellan had failed the test and had to be relieved.

After all the votes had been cast in the November 4, 1862, election, but before they had been tabulated, the formal order for McClellan's removal was drafted. While Lincoln realized that the country would not look positively on McClellan's removal, he also realized that the dismissal would not affect the outcome of the election. On November 7, Brigadier General Catherinus P. Buckingham left Washington to deliver the orders to McClellan. General Buckingham and General Ambrose E. Burnside met with McClellan around midnight. McClellan was handed two orders: one relieving him of command and the other appointing General Burnside as the new commander of the Army of the Potomac.

General McClellan took his removal well. He was reported to have said, in a rather pleasant tone, after reading both orders: "Well, Burnside, I turn command over to you." Burnside implored McClellan to stay with him for a few days to help ease the transition in command. McClellan agreed to stay on to help his old friend.[20]

On November 10, General McClellan met with his troops to bid them a final farewell. Even though the president had experienced difficulties with the general, McClellan was still extremely popular with the men. Many emotional scenes transpired during this final review. He was cheered and applauded by all the men who gathered. The Irish Brigade threw their colors in the dust. Some cried out, "Send him back! Send him back!" Many of the officers loudly expressed their desire for McClellan to put "himself at the head of the army and throw the infernal scoundrels at

Washington into the Potomac." Others yelled: "Lead us to Washington, General—we'll follow you!"[21] To McClellan's credit, all calls for insurrection were quickly dispelled by the former commander. The next day, McClellan left Warrenton for Washington. It was the last time the general was in the field during the war.

Burnside quickly took control in the Warrenton camp. He was required by the president to submit a plan for the movement of his forces. After a meeting with his makeshift staff on November 9, a plan was submitted to the president for approval. The specifics of the plan called for the abandonment of the present course toward Culpeper and Gordonsville, and proposed a new course toward Fredericksburg. Burnside believed that a quick movement in this direction would thwart Lee's efforts to consolidate his scattered forces. Burnside also reasoned that this plan would help secure the army's already strained supply lines. At that time, the army was using the Orange and Alexandria Railroad as its chief supply source. This new move would enable the military to use the Richmond, Fredericksburg and Potomac Railroad as its primary supply line, which would guarantee the security of the army. Two elements were necessary in order for this plan to succeed: rapid movement and pontoons. One of these worked to Burnside's advantage while the other did not.

During the days of strategic planning, the men of the 123rd remained in camp at Warrenton. On November 12, General Porter held a review to bid farewell to the V Corps. Similar to McClellan, Porter was relieved of command during the purge of the army and was temporarily replaced by General Joseph Hooker.

At this time, Burnside also reorganized the army for its upcoming campaign. He took the six infantry corps and consolidated them into three grand divisions of two corps each. General Joseph Hooker was appointed the commander of the Center Grand Division, which consisted of the III and V Corps. Upon his appointment as head of the Center Division, General Daniel Butterfield, a 31-year-old New York resident, was appointed commander of the V Corps. The Right Grand Division was commanded by General Edwin V. Sumner and consisted of the II and IX Corps. The Left Grand Division was led by General William B. Franklin and contained the I and VI Corps. Upon Burnside's completion of these adjustments, the command structure for the Fredericksburg campaign was set.

The men of the 123rd were oblivious to the shuffling of their commanders. On November 15, the Right Grand Division began its march to Fredericksburg. The next day, the men of the Left Grand Division left their camps and followed. All the while, the Center Grand Division remained in camp at Warrenton.

The following day, General Hooker held a grand review of his new division. Private Borland wrote that the 123rd was part of "a grand review of the division at 12 M. by Gen. Hooker, successor of Gen. Porter, commander of the center grand division of the Army of the Potomac."[22] Private Ross watched the event and noted that "[i]t was a pretty sight."[23] In the evening, the colonel conducted a service for the regiment and then informed the men that they would leave camp the next morning.

True to his word, at 8 A.M. on November 17, the regiment began its march south. The weather was not particularly co-operative, as the rain slowed the march. Private Ross wrote that "we did not get more than a mile from camp when we had to stop on account of the wagons."[24] Private Borland described the day's march as "a good march, considering the delays."[25] Overall, the regiment marched about 15 miles and camped for the night near Warrenton Junction.

The next day, November 18, the march began anew at 8 A.M. The regiment marched an estimated 18 miles, "the greater part of it done in the afternoon."[26] The 123rd camped for the night in an open field between Warrenton Junction and Falmouth. The men followed this routine of alternating between marching and camping for the next three days.

One of the key elements to the success of the campaign was a quick movement against Lee's isolated force at Fredericksburg. At the time when the march began, Fredericksburg was only occupied by four companies of Confederate infantry, a regiment of cavalry, and a light battery. As a result, on November 17, when General Sumner's Grand Division arrived on the river bank opposite Fredericksburg, the town was clearly held by an inferior force. The frustration for all concerned, however, was that the pontoons had not yet arrived.

Burnside was undoubtedly angered by this new turn of events. He had accomplished the first important step for the success of his campaign: rapidity of movement. The first elements of the army had traveled 36 miles from Warrenton to Fredericksburg in two days of hard marching. While Burnside had received his first inkling of a problem on November 14 when he learned that the pontoons had only then arrived in Washington, he was assured by the Union high command that the pontoons would be at his disposal, at the very latest, by November 17. But eight more days would transpire before the pontoons arrived at Fredericksburg. General Longstreet had arrived by that time and reinforced the small garrison at Fredericksburg; the tactical advantage had been lost.

Many of Burnside's commanders still felt that it was possible for the army to cross the river and occupy the city, even without the pontoons. On November 17, General Sumner strongly advocated this position. He reasoned that his men could wade across the river at the ford north of town and seize the high ground. General Burnside refused to permit this because of recent heavy rains. He believed the men would be trapped on the other side of the river if the ford flooded. Burnside decided to wait for the pontoons to arrive before attempting to cross the river.[27]

For the next eight days, the men on the heights opposite the town daily observed additional troops arriving at the city. At night, on the distant hills, an ever-increasing number of campfires could be seen. General Longstreet and his men arrived on November 19 and immediately began entrenching on the heights behind the town. Even though the Union army still had superior forces in the area, the Confederates were in control of the high ground.

The 123rd was not close enough to the town to witness the increasing Confederate activity. On November 22, the regiment moved its camp about six miles and camped near Falmouth in the area that had been occupied by the Pennsylvania Reserves during the summer of 1861. The regiment did not stay in this area for long, as they were ordered to pitch their tents in an area approximately one-half mile away. A letter to the *Chronicle* dated November 26 opined: "Our situation is not as desirable as could be wished for, owing to the insufficient supply of water and rails convenient to camp. We are distant about half a mile from Camp Beautiful, prepared by the Pennsylvania Reserves when under the command of Gen. McDowell, at this place."[28] The members of the 155th were equally as uncomplimentary about their new accommodations. Lieutenant D. Porter Marshall of Company K recalled that the new campsite was known as "Louse Hill." As he later described: "We had become well acquainted with that small insect generally called a grayback, which kept us on the move continually, when their namesakes over the line didn't."[29]

The men in the ranks were clearly unaware of the indecisiveness that was paralyzing the Union high command. Upon learning that Fredericksburg was occupied by additional forces, Burnside was vacillating as to what his next move would be. Because of the late arrival of the pontoons, a surprise move was clearly out of the question. Even after the pontoons arrived, Burnside waited another 18 days to make a decision. By that time, the Confederates had fortified the heights behind Fredericksburg into a nearly impregnable fortress.

During this period of time, the regiment lost four more of its members. The increasingly cold weather had taken its toll on the men of the unit. These deaths could be attributed to Humphreys' order that "no hospital tents [were] permitted to be erected whilst on the march." As one man sadly explained, "soldiers sick unto death [were] compelled to lay on the cold, damp ground having for a shelter only the small shelters in use by the men."[30]

Including these deaths, the regimental casualty list now numbered 14. Some other members remained hospitalized due to illness. Overall, the regiment had fared relatively well during its first four months of service. As a result, the Northern governors set aside the entire day of November 27 as a day of thanksgiving to God. This period of thanksgiving spilled over to November 28. While the men enjoyed this period of inactivity, General Burnside spent all of his time attempting to develop a new plan of attack.

It was clear to the general that the Confederates were fortifying the heights behind Fredericksburg. Although the pontoons had arrived, a direct assault on Fredericksburg appeared suicidal. Because of this, Burnside decided that it would be safer to cross the river several miles to the south at Skinker's Neck, an area within the range of Union gunboats. A reconnaissance of the area, however, revealed that the Confederates had a strong presence. With this option now out of the question, Burnside reasoned that his adversary must be weaker closer to the city and that an attack on the town was now his best option.

Yet from November 25 until December 9, Burnside wavered as to the exact plan and timing of the assault. Burnside finally made a decision at noon on December 9. He called his grand division commanders together and explained his plan. The scheme initially called for General Sumner to begin the attack by marching his grand division into Fredericksburg via the northern and middle pontoon bridges. Once his division had obtained control of the city and the river banks, General Hooker's Center Grand Division was to proceed across the same bridges. At that time, Sumner was to move his units forward and seize the heights over the Plank and Telegraph Roads. This ridge line, which consisted of Willis and Marye's Hills, would provide security for the remainder of the army as it crossed the river. General Hooker was to act as the reserve for Sumner and support his men during their attack on Marye's Heights.

Burnside also instructed Hooker that he was to be prepared to support the movements of General Franklin, who would cross his grand division over the southern bridges and move down the Old Richmond Road. Franklin was to attack the Confederate right flank and hopefully outflank the enemy's positions on the high ground of Marye's Heights. The commanders were told that they had the remainder of December 9 and the entire day of the 10th to prepare their men for the assault.

Following the meeting, General Sumner presented the plan to the subordinate generals of his grand division. Major General Darius Couch, the commander of the II Corps, was at the meeting and described the mood:

> . . . Sumner called a council to discuss what we were to do, the corps, division and brigade commanders were present. The result was a plain, free talk all around, in which words were not minced, for the conversation soon drifted into a marked disapprobation of the manner in which Burnside contemplated meeting the enemy . . . [T]here was not two opinions among the subordinate officers as to the rashness of the undertaking.[31]

General Couch was not the only individual who thought the strategy foolhardy. General Hooker freely criticized the plan. Many of the other commanders also expressed their opinion that Burnside was merely walking into Lee's trap.

General Burnside became aware of his comrades' misgivings on the evening of the 9th and called another meeting for December 10. General Couch related the substance of the meeting:

> He said he understood, in a general way, that we were opposed to his plans. He seemed to be rather severe on Hancock—to my surprise, for I did not think that officer had said as much as myself in opposition to the plan of attack. Burnside stated that he had formed his plans, and all he wanted was the devotion of the men. Hancock made a reply in which he disclaimed any discourtesy, and said he knew there was fortified heights on the opposite side, and that it would be pretty difficult for us to go over there and take them. I rose after him, knowing that I was the more guilty, and expressed a desire to serve Burnside, saying, among other things, that if I had ever done anything in battle, in this one I intended to do twice as much.[32]

While this debate was taking place, the men of the 123rd were beginning to wonder about the intentions of both armies. Private Hemphill wrote in a letter to his brother on December 1: "I can't understand the reason of both armies lying so close to each other so long without doing anything unless they are trying to make peace or something which I hope they will do before long."[33] Another member of the brigade also ruminated about the intentions of the armies. He believed that the armies would go into winter quarters. Considering the present location of the army, the soldier found such a prospect appealing:

> We have been near Fredericksburg for over two weeks, and instead of there being a prospect of a move, I am inclined to think we will winter here. We have everything necessary to make our present position comfortable through the long, dreary months of winter. Water is in abundance, clear as crystal; dense forests surround us capable of furnishing the necessary material for building purposes and for wood; a Government Railroad within one mile and a half, that can easily bring supplies from Aquia Creek . . .[34]

On December 9, the men began to receive information that a move was about to take place. Private Borland recorded: "Spent this forenoon on wood duty; our arms and accouterments were inspected by a U.S. inspecting officer; rumors of moving have been flying around camp yesterday and today, whether founded on fact I can not say, time that never failing arbiter will tell."[35]

The regiment received orders to begin preparations for the march on December 10. They "[s]pent [the day] writing letters, cooking rations" and preparing themselves for the "mortal combat" that lay ahead.[36] There were rumors that the regiment was to cross the river the following day.[37] The company commanders directed the men to cook three days' rations and have all their personal effects ready for a move. All of the men were ordered to carry 60 rounds of ammunition: 40 for their cartridge boxes and 20 for their pockets.

The regiment was undoubtedly anxious and apprehensive about entering battle. They were concerned about the Confederate activity at Fredericksburg but were resigned to their duty. As one man later wrote: "At the camps on both sides of the Rappahannock, veterans settled down to get what rest they could, while young recruits wondered how they would like their first 'look at the elephant.'"[38]

The Union engineers began the task of assembling the pontoon bridges over the Rappahannock on December 11. Five bridges were constructed across the river to facilitate the movement of the troops. The construction of the bridges was not an easy task as Mississippi sharpshooters were picking off the Union engineers. As a result, the bridge construction was brought to a standstill.

Burnside had anticipated that the crossing would be completed during the early hours of December 11. But by noon of that day, only the lower bridges opposite Deep Run were completed. This unanticipated complication pushed back Burnside's timetable, leaving him little options but to shell the town. Therefore, at about 12:30 P.M., Burnside ordered 183 pieces to begin the cannonade. As one soldier later wrote: "[This] began what was probably the most concentrated bombardment of such a small target ever to be made in the United States."[39]

As the above action unfolded, the members of the 123rd prepared for their move to the battlefield. The regiment was awakened at 4 A.M. and ordered to be in line at first light. At about 8 A.M., the group formed on the parade ground and marched about three miles in "ankle deep" mud toward the town. During the entire time, the men could hear the "heavy and incessant" bombardment of the town and "the whistling of the shells" as they headed toward their destination.[40] When the march ended, the regiment was halted in the rear of the firing batteries, where they lay for the remainder of the day and night.

Chaplain Andrew J. Hartsock of the 133rd told of the surrealistic night scene experienced by the men:

> Tonight I saw the sun set in the smoke of battle. It surpassed any thing I had ever imagined. The rolling sound of heavy artillery, the imagination of the bombardment of

Fredericksburg, the darkened heavens, the sun setting in blood, truly a fitting appearance for the orb of day that looked down upon the crimson tide that flowed from American veins. The smoke upon the sky at Sunset formed the back ground of the picture. Then was seen the burning fuse of the shell as lightning passing over the heavens. Now a shell explodes upon that back ground and forms most beautiful wreaths. The changing colors, the different scenes, formed the most beautiful, and sublime view that the eye could desire.[41]

During the later part of the afternoon on December 11, the pontoon bridges were finally completed. At approximately 4:30 P.M., the II Corps began its crossing of the river. Upon entering the town, the men observed that the Union bombardment had destroyed many of the town's finest structures. Fires from the bombardment were still smoldering, creating a strange and eerie scene. A *New York Times* correspondent described the area: "In some cases the whole side of a house has been shot away, roofs and chimneys have tumbled in, window frames smashed to atoms, and doors jarred from the hinges. Huge limbs have been shot away from the shade trees . . . the ancient and aristocratic town of Fredericksburg never looked so seedy as it did after our batteries had done with it to-night."[42]

The doors to the finest homes were knocked down and the contents stolen. Vases, lamps, and other personal objects were indiscriminately broken. A chaplain for a Connecticut regiment reported seeing a cavalry man sit down "at a fine rosewood piano" and drive "his saber through the polished keys." The same individual also told of a soldier who "entered a large parlor carpeted with a large Brussels worth at least two hundred dollars," who "cut out the center-piece . . . for a saddle blanket." A Union artillery lieutenant, whose battery had caused much of the destruction, concluded: "I never felt so much disgusted with the war as I did that day. I wish that the war could be brought to an end and put a stop to all this terrible suffering."[43]

The men of the 123rd did not participate in this wanton destruction. Throughout the afternoon of the 11th, the regiment remained on the northern side of the Rappahannock. At four o'clock the next morning, they started to move toward the river but did not cross it. By nightfall of the 12th, the Right and Left Grand Divisions had, for all practical purposes, completed their crossings. Hooker's Center Grand Division was the only large force that remained on the northern side.

Reports just prior to the battle reflect that the Right and Left Grand Divisions had approximately 23,000 and 43,000 men fit for duty respectively.[44] Considering that close to 66,000 men were huddled in the cramped environs around Fredericksburg, it is little wonder that Hooker's Grand Division remained on the northern side of the river.

The problems that the army had experienced on December 11 in the bridging of the Rappahannock had pushed back the preestablished timetable almost 24 hours. Because of this, Lee was further able to consolidate his scattered forces and strengthen his already impregnable position. Faced with this dilemma, Burnside had only three real choices. First, he could move the army south along the banks of the Rappahannock in hopes of outflanking Lee by moving around his right flank. Second, he could cancel the entire operation and recross his army back to the northern side of the river and go into winter quarters. Third, and the only viable option left, was to attempt a frontal assault against Lee's forces. While conventional wisdom was against such a move, Burnside opted for this choice.[45]

According to Burnside's plan, General Franklin and his grand division were to attack the Confederate right flank on Prospect Hill and take this area. Once this was accomplished, the army would be in position to outflank the Confederate positions on both the center and left of the line. If this initial attack succeeded, Burnside envisioned that the right grand division would assault the Confederate positions on Marye's Heights. With this position now untenable due to the collapse of the Confederate right flank, the Union army could easily take the heights. General Hooker's division was to be held in reserve to aid either Franklin or Sumner, as necessary. This plan of attack was conveyed to the commanders of the divisions in the early morning hours of December 13—the great battle was about to begin.

Chapter Three
Battle of Fredericksburg

Yea though I walk through the Valley of the Shadow of Death, I will fear no evil . . .

The soldiers of the 123rd were awakened at 4 A.M. on the day of the battle. As the men began to prepare their morning coffee, many could not help but think about the daunting task that lay ahead. The engagement was to be the regiment's baptism of fire, and none of the men knew how they would act. Since the regiment had its origins in the basement of a church, many of the men put their faith in God. John C. Anderson, a second lieutenant in Company I, summed up the feelings of most of the men: "I was fully prepared in my own mind to meet whatever was my lot as I cast my soul and body into the care of him who never forsakes those who put their trust in him . . ."[1]

As the regiment watched night turn to day, the first light revealed a thick fog shrouding the fields around Fredericksburg. The fog was so thick that the conflicting armies were "completely veiled from each other's sight." The impregnable mist made visibility so difficult that "nothing could be seen at a distance of ten or twelve rods."[2]

At daylight, the 123rd fell in and advanced to the position it held on the previous day near the Phillips House. Private Ross explained:

> Just received orders to fall in. We marched out of the forest to the same place we lay yesterday. Formed and we are waiting for our turn to cross. From the firing that is going on now, I think there must be a battle going on; about 9 o'clock we could hear distinctly the sharp fire of musketry, not long afterwards commenced the heavy roar of artillery. It is now

52

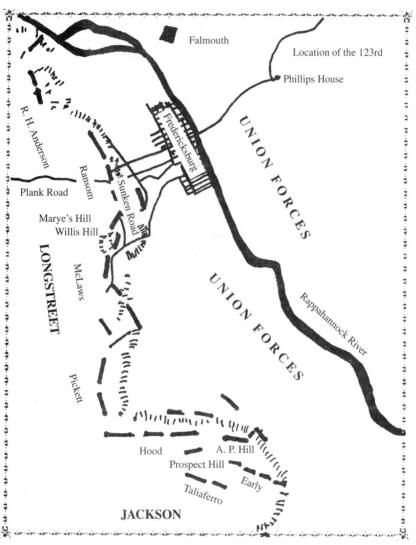

Falmouth

Location of the 123rd

Phillips House

R. H. Anderson

UNION FORCES

Fredericksburg

Ransom

Sunken Road

Plank Road

Marye's Hill
Willis Hill

LONGSTREET

McLaws

UNION FORCES

Rappahannock River

Pickett

UNION FORCES

Hood

A. P. Hill

Prospect Hill

Early

Taliaferro

JACKSON

Troop Positions Evening of December 12 and Morning of December 13

10 o'clock and the firing is still going on, but is farther down the river. Sounds as though the enemy were falling or being driven back.[3]

The initial sounds Private Ross heard came from the vicinity of Prospect Hill. The first prong of Burnside's plan called for General Franklin to attack the Confederate right flank. The action in this area commenced at about 10:00 A.M. General George Meade's division assaulted the Confederate flank and had some early success in breaching the line. Private Ross' observation that the "enemy was falling or being driven back" was correct, although the timing appears to be a little premature.

After Franklin's attack on the Confederate right, but before any word of its success or failure reached the Union high command, General Burnside ordered General Sumner to begin his attack against the Confederate center. By giving this order, Burnside abandoned his original plan of attack. According to his original plan, Sumner was only to attack the heights after General Franklin had successfully collapsed the Confederate right. Unfortunately, General Burnside's impatience persuaded him to proceed with these attacks without any further word from the Union left. This precipitous order set in motion a series of disastrous events that ultimately culminated with the involvement of the 123rd.

At the time of the battle, Fredericksburg was a small town nestled on the banks of the Rappahannock. The majority of the town's buildings rested within a few hundred yards of the river. The ground west of town, where the Confederate center was entrenched, was largely an open tract of land divided by a number of fences. Although a number of homes were scattered throughout the area, the ground was largely an unpopulated expanse.

The first obstacle encountered in this expanse was a mill-race or canal located at the foot of a gradual upward slope. One narrow wooden bridge spanned the waterway.[4] However, the millrace was only five feet deep and fifteen feet wide, so it could easily be waded.

After crossing the millrace, about 30 to 50 feet ahead, was a small bench or terrace. The ground from the edge of the mill-race to the bench formed an embankment which partially hid any person or unit forming in this area.[5] In the 250 yards from the bench to the base of Willis and Marye's Hills, a number of structures were visible and would play a prominent role in the battle.

A small brick house, known as the Stratton House, stood 150 yards up the slope. To the north of the house, approximately the same distance, was the Stratton Wheelwright Shop.[6] Fifty feet farther west toward the hills was a small depression which was approximately 18 inches deep.

One hundred yards ahead was the Telegraph Road, which ran along the base of Willis Hill and Marye's Hill. The road in this area had been cut from the edge of the ridge line and was below the surrounding plain. Stone walls had been built on each side of the roadway and formed a ready-made entrenchment for any defending army. This area was known as the sunken road.

At the southern end of Marye's Hill along the Telegraph Road stood the Hall House. Also along the Telegraph Road, farther north, was the Stephens House. The Innis House was located next to the Stephens House. Across the Telegraph Road the ground sloped sharply upward to the crest of both hills. Willis Hill, the more southern hill, had three structures and a cemetery occupying its heights. Marye's Hill had probably the most famous structure, Brompton, at or near its crest.[7]

Two images have been found which help in conceptualizing this area. The most striking aspect of the first image is the open space between the town and the heights. While there were two spots which helped to conceal the attacking columns (the small depression around the brick house and the bench near the mill-race), the picture shows the unprotected expanse that the troops had to travel.

The second image is a panoramic view of the battlefield that was taken on May 19, 1863, during the Wilderness and Spotsylvania Campaigns. The image demonstrates the openness

Stratton House
A larger section of the picture on page 61 shows how the house appeared in 1864. Many of the men referred to the structure as the "Brick House."
MOLLUS-MASS

Stratton's Wheelwright Shop
A larger picture on page 60 shows how the buildings appeared to the 123rd.
Anne S. K. Brown Collection, Brown University Library

Innis House
The house was filled with Confederate sharpshooters on the day of the battle.
The house still stands today.

Stephens House
Another house used by Confederate sharpshooters.

Hall House
The modern day Visitor's Center sits where the Hall House stood in December of 1862. The men of the 123rd saw this house directly ahead.

Brompton
Home of the Marye family. Many bullets from the battle are still lodged in the bricks.

of the plain to the west of Fredericksburg. The Stratton House can clearly be seen in the middle background. Hanover Street is to the right of the photograph image. While some undulations in the terrain can be noted, the quality of the print does not afford the best view of the two known depressions.

General Couch's II Corps was the first to attack the Confederate center. At approximately 12 noon, General Couch's Third Division, commanded by General William H. French, received orders to begin the first of many attacks on the stone wall. The men moved forward with high hopes of carrying the wall. They advanced on the double-quick, with bayonets fixed, toward the Confederate line. As the men began their climb, Confederate artillery opened a deadly fire. Not a single shot was fired by the column. When they were within one hundred yards of the wall, the Confederate infantry delivered a volley which caused the line to waver.[8] Confederate sharpshooters in the Innis and Stephens Houses were picking off the men with deadly accuracy.[9] General Couch watched the action from a church steeple in town and sadly saw his men being cut down. He could not help but exclaim to General Oliver Howard: "Oh great God! see how our men, our poor fellows are falling!"[10]

The men tried to rally but the Confederate line was too strong. Confusion reigned on the field as each man attempted to save himself. Those who could run sought shelter in the houses on the hill. The Stratton House was filled to capacity and provided safety for the living, as well as the wounded. Others who could walk limped back to the millrace. All in all, General French's Division lost 1,160 men in their assault upon the heights.[11]

Even with this first inkling of disaster, Burnside committed Couch's second division to the attack. The Confederates, seeing another attacking column moving toward the heights, sent new regiments to bolster their defense.[12] With this increased musket fire, more and more men fell before the wall. In the 5th New Hampshire, 17 of the 23 officers and 165 of the 280 enlisted men were either killed or wounded during the assault. None in the division were able to reach the wall, as over 2,000 more men joined the casualty ranks.[13]

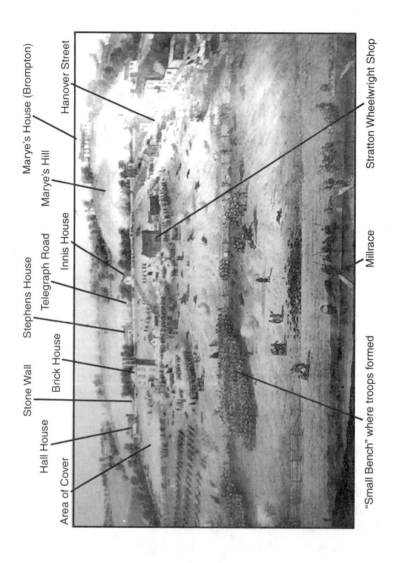

Hall House
Stone Wall
Stephens House
Brick House
Telegraph Road
Innis House
Marye's House (Brompton)
Marye's Hill
Hanover Street
Area of Cover
"Small Bench" where troops formed
Millrace
Stratton Wheelwright Shop

Charge of Kimball's Brigade in the Battle of Fredericksburg,
Saturday, December 13, 1862

A panoramic drawing of how the area appeared to the men of the 123rd. (Colored lithograph
by P. S. Duval & Son [Philadelphia] after J. G. Keyser, 1863)

Anne S. K. Brown Military Collection, Brown University Library

Open expanse the men had to cross

Stratton House ("Brick House")

Stone Wall

Marye's House (Brompton)

View of Marye's Heights Looking West from Fredericksburg
Picture taken in May of 1864 from the town of Fredericksburg, looking toward Marye's Heights.

MOLLUS-MASS.

General Oliver O. Howard and his three brigades were the last II Corps division ordered into the fray. The men of these brigades made a number of bold attempts to take the enemy's works, "but the concentrated fire of artillery and infantry was too much to carry the men through."[14] General Howard's division lost 914 men (104 killed, 718 wounded, and 92 captured or missing) before their day's work was complete.[15] The total casualties in General Couch's corps totaled 4,106 men. This should have been considered by General Burnside before any further assaults were attempted. But the general gave the matter no thought. His only concern was the taking of the hill which could only be accomplished by the commitment of more troops.

With this in mind, General Burnside gave the order for General Orlando B. Willcox's IX Corps to continue the offensive. General Samuel D. Sturgis' second division was chosen as the assaulting force. The results for this division were as disastrous as the others. General Willcox wrote: "All these troops behaved well and marched under a heavy fire across the broken plain, pressed up to the enemy's sloping crest, and maintained every inch of ground with great obstinacy until after nightfall, but the position could not be carried."[16] After Sturgis' assault, the casualty total rose again. Sturgis' division added another 1,007 men to the ever-increasing number (94 killed, 827 wounded, and 86 captured or missing).[17] Even more frustrating was the fact that the over 5,000 casualties had accomplished nothing. At around two o'clock, General Hooker received orders from General Burnside to send one of his divisions to support the attack that was being made by General Sturgis. General Charles Griffin's division, of the V Corps, was sent to Sturgis' aid.

At the same time, General Burnside also ordered General Hooker to bring his other two divisions (Humphreys' and Sykes') across the river to support the renewed attacks. After receiving the order, General Hooker sent his aide to the commanding general to advise him that any further attacks in the area would be disastrous. Even after watching the carnage from the window of his headquarters, General Burnside insisted that the attack must take place.[18] Believing that he could personally dissuade the general, General Hooker went over to headquarters and argued his case. But Burnside still insisted that the assault had to be made.[19] This chain of events put the 123rd in motion.

It is not exactly clear when the regiment actually began its march to the field. The earliest time mentioned appeared in a letter from R. W. Bard of Company H to his father. In that letter, the sergeant placed the time at noon.[20] There is no other evidence that the regiment made its final move to the field at this early hour. There are a number of individuals who did report, however, that the division made a short move around this time. Chaplain Hartsock of the 133rd placed the move at 1 P.M. But under either time frame, the men marched for a short distance and stopped near the Phillips House, in an area that overlooked the battlefield. There they caught the first glimpse of a Civil War battle. The distant fields were covered with smoke and the sounds of musketry and artillery could be heard. They could see that the rebel army was "intrenched on the heights beyond the city,"[21] but they did not yet know that they would be called upon to attack this intrenched position.

As the men gathered around the Phillips House, Colonel Allabach told them: "It now remains for us to cross the river, make the final charge, and carry the position. I wish every man to do his duty." General Humphreys offered the men further motivation: "Soldiers, you are the reserve division of the army. Yonder [pointing to the batteries] are the enemy batteries. It remains with you to go in and take them and the day is won. Forward!"[22]

With these words of encouragement, the 123rd, along with the 131st, 133rd, and 155th, moved down the hill from Stafford Heights to begin crossing the Rappahannock on the upper pontoon bridges. The early morning fog had disappeared by this time and the haze and "smoke did not obstruct the view" of the enemy's artillery. Earlier in the day, the Confederate fire "had very poor range," but as the "Division was getting into line and marching down the hillside to the pontoon approaches, the shells had better range."[23]

Although they were under constant shelling, there were no reports of any men breaking ranks, but "in crossing the pontoons, the troops experienced a singular sensation. The fact that one's chances of being killed or drowned if wounded and knocked off the pontoons into the stream was far from consoling. Officers and men, however, recognized the dilemma and hurried across, not a halt occurring during the passage."[24] The shots and shells were coming "uncomfortably close" as the troops rushed across the pontoons.[25] Christian Rhein of Company B remembered: "Johnnies got a good range on the bridge from Marye's Heights, and were sending shells shrieking towards us with more success than pleased us."[26]

This artillery barrage was the brigade's first experience in battle. L. Brackenridge, an orderly sergeant in the 123rd, described the sensation a short time after the battle: "One week ago yesterday our division crossed a pontoon bridge into the city of Fredericksburg, the shells and bullets whistling over our heads like hail. Every bullet made us dodge our heads and keep the ranks closed."[27] Chaplain Hartsock of the 133rd recounted that the sound of the shelling was "terrifying" and "shock[ed] the nervous system."[28]

Many of the men, after this initial baptism of fire, vowed to ignore the constant shelling. But these pledges were soon forgotten. Chaplain Hartsock spoke of his own personal experience:

> The farther we advanced the faster and closer they came, striking all around us. When we entered the Pontoon Bridge it was terrible . . . I cannot describe my feelings while on the Pontoons, they were not the most pleasant of my life . . . The shrieking of the shells would alarm me to a certain extent . . . At first when a shell would come near me I would dodge. I remembered the speech I had made the Reg., how I urged them to be brave and now I was dodging [shellfire] . . . I braced myself in the stirrups and determined that I would not dodge if it took my life, but soon another [shell] came near me and I instinctively dodged. It is natural to dodge the shells . . . [W]e all dodged.[29]

Fortunately for the 123rd, not a single member of the regiment was injured in the crossing. Second Lieutenant S. D. Karns of Company I, who would be wounded in the subsequent assault, told of the miraculous crossing: "The regiment, while crossing the pontoon bridge into Fredericksburg, was shelled by the rebel batteries. The shells exploded about the regiment, and fell in the water near the bridge, but, singular as it may appear, not a man was injured."[30]

Upon reaching the other side, the regiment rested for a few minutes in the streets near the Rappahannock and lay down to keep clear of the bullets. The shots and shells were pouring in at a furious rate as soldiers from other units could be seen everywhere. Some were wounded and seeking shelter from death, while others were running from the hailstorm ahead. But the men of the 123rd found shelter, wherever they could, and waited for their next move.

In short order, the men received orders to proceed to the battlefield. General Humphreys "received an urgent request from Major General Couch to support that part of his corps on the left of the Telegraph [Hanover] road . . ."[31] The reason for the immediacy of Couch's order was not initially known to General Humphreys. But like another great charge that would transpire in less than seven months at Gettysburg, the precipitousness of the movement was based on a misinterpretation of the enemies' intentions.

Prior to General Couch's order, a group of Hancock's men had informed Generals Couch and Hancock that they had observed a Confederate battery retiring from the heights. This retrograde movement was interpreted by the generals as a sign that the Confederates were retiring from the hill. This belief led Couch to emphatically tell Humphreys, "Now is the time for you to go in!"[32] The 123rd was put in motion.

The brigade moved forward on two separate roads. The 155th and the 123rd began their advance westward on Fauquier Street while the men of the 131st and 133rd traveled on a parallel street. This group marched up one block to the intersection of Fauquier and Caroline Streets. The men made a left on Caroline Street and marched five blocks to the intersection of Hanover Street. At Hanover Street, the men turned right and met the other two regiments for their final march to the field.

At this point in the trek, the men could see firsthand the effects of the prior days' bombardment. At the first intersection on Hanover Street, the regiment observed the courthouse and St. George's Episcopal Church. A photograph taken in the spring of 1863 illustrates how the area appeared to the 123rd.

The regiment continued to the intersection of Hanover and Liberty Streets where they began to deploy for their final assault on Marye's Heights. In the top photograph on page 67, the regiment would have been marching up the street, entering at the right of the picture. Farther to the right, out of camera view, was the area where the men began to align for the assault. The men crossed the millrace and began to form "under the brow of a hill

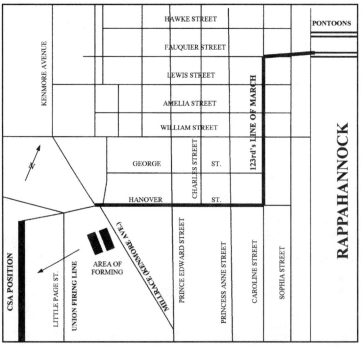

Modern Map
Line of march to the field by the 123rd.

Hanover and Liberty Streets on the Battlefield

The Courthouse and St. George's Episcopal Church
Looking North on Princess Street

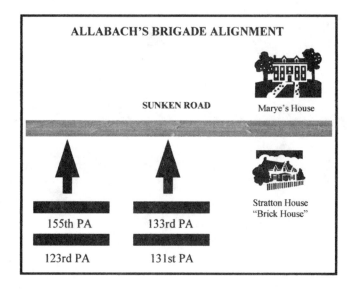

in front of the enemies works."[33] This brow or bench afforded the brigade some partial cover while forming.

The men had a brief moment, while stowing their knapsacks, to look over the field. Directly ahead lay the heights the men were ordered to assault. The rank and file gave their first impressions of the field. Corporal Henry F. Weaver, a member of the 155th, wrote:

> There comes our first realization of war and battle. Outside the cellar and laying on the earth thrown from it are our killed and wounded, the piteous appeals of the latter being enough to appall and shock the stoutest hearts unused to such scenes. We would not fain help them if we could, but a rigorous and relentless enemy in front is engrossing all our thoughts and time now.[34]

Chaplain Hartsock only noted: "I cannot describe the awful scenes of butchery. Men mangled and torn in every part, ah terrible war."[35]

There was little time to linger over the carnage since the men needed to prepare for the upcoming assault. The brigade was formed in two lines at close distance; the 155th on the left, the 133rd on the right, the 123rd to the rear of the 155th, and the 131st to the rear of the 133rd.[36]

While the brigade was deploying, all available batteries were bombarding the Confederate works in the hopes of creating a hole in the enemy's defenses for the attack. Two batteries were placed on the left of the road, within four hundred yards of the Confederate position, with the parts of other batteries posted on the right. The artillery fired vigorously on the Confederate position, ceasing just before the commencement of Humphreys' assault.[37]

The 123rd aligned in the traditional battle formation. Companies B, G, K, E, and H formed the left wing of the regiment while Companies C, I, D, F, and A formed the right. Under this alignment, the major and the lieutenant colonel were 8 paces behind the second rank, and the colonel 30 paces behind. It has been reported that General Humphreys ordered the regimental officers to the front, prior to Allabach's assault. This author contends that during this initial phase of the attack, all officers remained in their traditional battle alignments.[38] It is clear, after this initial assault, that Humphreys did in fact order the officers to the front. A participant in the charge made by Tyler's men, the brigade that made its assault after Allabach's, recalled that the general's "command rang out loud and firm, 'Officers to the front in this charge. Never mind the obstacles in the way! Charge!'"[39] A member of his staff also humorously remembered that "General Humphreys—always a very *polite* man—turned around to [us], and in his blandest manner remarked 'Young gentleman, I intend to lead this assault, and shall be happy to have the pleasure of your company.'" The staff member concluded that "[o]f course the invitation was too polite to be declined."[40] But there is no evidence to indicate that the officers were anywhere but in their traditional battle positions during Allabach's initial assault.

As noted above, General Humphreys was described by one of his subordinates as a polite man on the day of the battle. Colonel Edward J. Allen of the 155th had a far different opinion of his commander. The cause for this discrepancy involved General Humphreys' displeasure over Colonel Allen's detailing of six of the "youngest and least sturdy looking boys" as guards for the regiment's knapsacks. General Humphreys discovered these men,

123rd Pennsylvania Volunteers
Regimental Alignment

Confederate Forces

Right Wing

Co. C	Co. I	Co. D	Co. F	Co. A
Adams	Humes	Tyler	Boyd	Wiley

Left Wing

Co. B	Co. G	Co. K	Co. E	Co. H	Colors
Murphy	Boisol	Maxwell	Bell	Drum	

Lt. Col. (Position was vacant as Lt. Col. Frederick Gast was under arrest.)

William P. McNary Adj.

Hugh Danver Maj.

Bascom Smith (8 paces back) Sgt. Maj.

(12 paces back) Franklin Bailey QM Sgt.

(30 paces back) John B. Clark Col.

just before the charge, and "indignantly and profanely order[ed] . . . the knapsack guard to report at once to their companies, insinuating most unjustly that they were a lot of skulkers."[41] Two of these "skulkers" paid the ultimate price and were killed in the charge.

One final order was issued by General Humphreys before the men left the safety of the ravine. The general ordered his adjutant to tell Colonel Allabach that the assault was to be made with all muskets unloaded. General Humphreys emphatically told his adjutant: "McClellan, the bayonet is the only thing that will do any good here."[42] When the order was given, the men were confused. They expected to be told, at any moment, to load their muskets.[43] Instead, Allabach had the brigade ring their rifles to prove they were unloaded. The men would make the assault with the bayonet alone. With this final preparation complete, Allabach directed the front line at charge bayonets and the second line at right shoulder arms.[44] The "forlorn hope," a term used by General Hooker for Humphreys' assault, was ready to move.

The order to move rang out loud and clear and the men moved out from the protective bench near the millrace.[45] Colonel Clark watched his men move forward "in one beautiful line."[46] The men continued up the hill to the meadow. One member of the brigade noted: "Nothing could be more perfect than the line of the four regiments as they advance . . . We have been in many dress parades and regimental drills, but have never in any of them seen a more splendid formation than that which now presents itself as the lines advance with their colors—*those glorious colors of the Union and the State of Pennsylvania!*"[47]

General Hooker witnessed the initial movement of the brigade and was also impressed with the formation of the men. "When the word was given the men moved forward with great impetuosity. They ran and hurrahed and I was encouraged by the great feeling that pervaded them."[48] Another member of the division said it was "like the onrushing of a tornado through some rocky canyon."[49]

Observations were not only made by the Union army; the enemy was equally impressed with the formation. Private

Alexander Hill of the 17th Virginia Infantry recalled the awe-inspiring scene:

> Just before sunset, everything being quiet along the line, many of the reserve, without orders, crowded to the front and were spectators of that last forlorn hope led by gallant Humphries [*sic*] . . . From the hill back of the heights the division of Pickett watched the advance, filled with wonder and a pitying admiration for men who could rush with such unflinching valor, such mad recklessness into the jaws of destruction . . . Across the plain, with no martial music to thrill them, only a stillness that would strike terror into spirits less gallant—across the plain still onward sweeps the dauntless brigade with serried lines and gleaming steel. It was superb.[50]

While this spectacle was clearly a "superb" sight, the undeniable truth was that the brigade was now moving into the open. For most of the attacking column this was the first time they had a clear view of the ground ahead. What these soldiers observed would have undoubtedly unnerved the most seasoned veterans. Everywhere in their front were the dead and wounded from prior assaults. Thousands of their comrades, remnants of at least 20 regiments, were clinging desperately to the hill for cover. Except for the troopers who were standing behind the Stratton House or its outbuildings, all others were prone. Officers and enlisted personnel were lying together, hugging the earth to survive. Fallen horses could be seen with men huddled between their legs for shelter. Many were lying behind whatever rocks they could find. Some even observed their dead comrades being used as shelter against the fire from the hill.[51]

Amazingly enough, even after observing these chaotic conditions, the line never faltered. The commanders and their subordinates continued to move steadily toward the wall. General Humphreys proudly watched as the soldiers from the 123rd "moved rapidly and gallantly up to General Couch's troops," under the "artillery and musketry fire of the enemy."[52]

Humphreys' Attack

The charge of Humphreys' Division as seen through the artistry of Alfred Waud. The 123rd would be to the left in the picture in the second line.

After the line marched approximately 250 yards, and as they moved closer to the wall, the order was given: "Advance! Double Quick!" toward the wall.[53] The beautiful line that had characterized the beginning of the march slowly began to disappear. "All order, all formation — in fact, all discipline — disappeared amidst the smoke and fire of battle, every man was for the moment his own commander."[54] The situation was further complicated by the loss of the regiment's third in command, Major Hugh Danver. The major was not hit by any gunfire or shrapnel but was spitting up blood, due to a chronic lung condition, as the unit approached the wall.[55] This loss did little to soothe the already tattered nerves of the men in the regiment. Gone was the calming influence of the fatherly butcher from Allegheny. But the men never wavered as they continued to move forward toward the enemy ahead.

Within the next few yards, the unit reached the line of troops lying prostrate on the hill. This disorganized mass of men was "probably six or eight ranks deep."[56] These men posed a serious obstacle to the men of the brigade. Not only did they form a physical obstruction to the movement of the brigade, they also created a psychological barrier to Allabach's men. One colonel of the brigade wrote: "My men, not knowing that they should pass over this line, covered themselves as well as they could in the rear of the line."[57] General Humphreys wholeheartedly agreed with the colonel and noted in his after-battle report: "Finding [these men] lying there, the men of Allabach's brigade, who had never been in battle before, instinctively followed their example. Besides, they disordered my lines and were greatly in the way when I wished to bring the brigade to a charge."[58]

Psychologically, the damage done by these troops may well have been greater. These seasoned veterans cried out to Humphreys' men, "lie down—you will all be killed."[59] Others caught at their legs as they passed, attempting to hold them back. One private of the brigade was caught by a member of the 5th New Hampshire who "pulled [his] overcoat skirt violently and motioned [for him] to lay down."[60] A good many of the men in the brigade followed this example and lay down.

Colonel Allabach, mindful of this problem, attempted to have the other divisions' men withdrawn. He rode "off to the right and . . . found an officer" whom he asked "to withdraw his men."[61] The officer refused the request. General Humphreys was fuming over his brigades' inability to move forward. He later offered an opinion on this manmade barrier: "I cannot refrain from expressing my opinion that one of the greatest obstacles to my success was the mass of troops lying out front. They ought to have been withdrawn before mine advanced."[62] Unfortunately for General Humphreys and this brigade it was too late.

The line was now within one hundred yards of the wall. The men were lying with the dead and dying of the prior assaults. The corpses that covered the ground were in "constant motion from the kick of rebel bullets striking them." Some of these poor unfortunates were "cut to tatters."[63] Lieutenant John Anderson of Company I saw his messmate, Johnny McIntire, shot by his side. He felt it was time "to avenge his & others deaths."[64]

The men began to fire at the enemy ahead in an alternating pattern of loading while lying down and standing to fire.[65] The column "was a steady stream of musketry, but the powder used was so inferior that it fouled the barrels and made reloading very laborious."[66] The standing to fire led one soldier to witness "fifteen men within a circle of twenty feet" be either killed or wounded.[67] Even more frustrating was the realization that the firing was having little effect on the enemy. The bullets that did manage to reach the enemy "could be . . . distinctly [heard] spattering against the stone wall."[68]

After closely observing the situation, General Humphreys knew that the only way to carry the heights "was with the bayonet." Orders were given down the line for each regiment to cease firing, but once received, were not quickly followed. Only after General Humphreys, Colonel Allabach, Colonel Allen of the 155th, Colonel Clark, and Captain Horatio K. Tyler walked the line, telling each man individually to cease firing, was the shooting arrested.[69]

General Humphreys ordered the officers of the brigade to the front. The general sat on his horse to the rear of the men, "looking cross and savage" as orders rang out for the advance.[70] He ordered the men: "Damn it [do] not waste so much ball—give them the cold steel—thats what the rascals want."[71] Three times the order to advance was given. On the third order, the "line of the brigade started forward."[72]

The line steadily moved forward toward the wall "under a galling fire of musketry and grape."[73] The right wing companies of the 123rd were hit especially hard. The left wing companies had difficulty moving forward because they were "partly enveloped by the One Hundred and Fifty-fifth," which was partially blocked by parts of two other regiments.[74] The men of the 155th clearly empathized with their brigade comrades:

> Grape, canister and minie balls are poured into us from the enemy's artillery and infantry. We are, in a sense, powerless. While our Regiment escapes to the extent the full force of the terrible artillery fire, owing to the range being a little high, after the fact that the rebels have withdrawn their batteries to the right of our front from which they poured a merciless cross-fire upon the One Hundred and Twenty-third and other regiments in our Brigade, which suffered terribly.[75]

As a result, three of the five company commanders of the right wing were wounded.[76] In Company I, all of the officers were either killed or wounded.[77] The regimental colors, on the extreme left of the right wing, were pierced by twelve bullets and the wooden staff splintered by the thirteenth.[78]

As the men moved within 50 yards of the wall, a quintuple line of Confederates rose up and delivered a withering fire. The batteries on the hill were shooting double canister as the first line faltered, then stopped.[79] As the second line, which contained the 123rd, moved forward, the musketry and artillery fire increased. The "fated dead line" had been reached and the men valiantly attempted to cross. Similar to the first wave of the attack, the line was "impossible to pass."[80] With the line "all cut to pieces," the men had no choice but to seek the safety of the hill.[81] Colonel Allabach watched the charge "press . . . forward to within 12 paces of the stone wall," then fall back to "the line of the second formation."[82] General Couch witnessed the assault and wrote: "The musketry fire was heavy, and the artillery fire was simply terrible. I sent word several times to our artillery on the right of Falmouth that they were firing into us, and were tearing our men to pieces. I thought they had made a mistake in the range. But I learned later that the fire came from the guns of the enemy on the extreme left."[83]

As General Humphreys and his staff began the charge on horseback, many horses were shot down. Humphreys revealed his own experience: "I had two horses shot down under me. My horse Charley was twice wounded and had but three legs to limp on. I took the orderly's horse; he was killed under me in fifteen minutes. It was a perfect hailstorm of bullets for an hour and a half . . . Every officer in my staff except two had their horses shot under them."[84] Amazingly enough, General Humphreys did not receive a scratch in the engagement.

During the last assault, General Humphreys was in the general vicinity of the 123rd. In his after-battle report, he spoke highly of Colonel Clark, and particularly of Captain Tyler of Company D, for their contributions in the attack. He wrote of the "cool courage of . . . Colonel Clark" and specifically commended Captain Tyler for his help in "bringing the brigade to a charge." He concluded these commendations by noting that these officers were "particularly under my own observation, and I desire to bring their conduct to your notice."[85]

The true strength of Captain Tyler's company, at the time of the assault, is not exactly known. It is known, however, that General Humphreys stated in his report that the division mustered 4,500 men on the day of the fight. Based on the assumption that this number was evenly spread out over the eight regiments in the brigade, the 123rd would have had approximately 560 men fit for duty. If this number was also equally spread out over the companies in the regiment, then Captain Tyler would have mustered about 56 men for the assault. While there is some discrepancy in the number of casualties received by the regiment, it

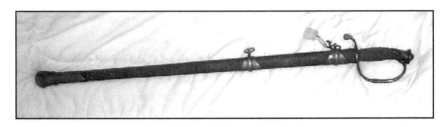

Captain Tyler's Sword
The commander of Company D was wounded during the assault carrying this sword.

Lang Collection

appears very likely that Tyler's company had close to a 50 per-cent casualty rate.[86]

In total, the regiment had 135 casualties. Based on the assumption that the effective strength of the regiment totaled 560, the unit would have had nearly a 25 percent casualty rate.[87] Even though all prior units had failed in their attempts to take the heights, Humphreys was ordered to send in Tyler's brigade. There was a short lull in the attack while Tyler's brigade readied itself for the assault.

The men of Allabach's brigade watched helplessly as their divisional comrades were called to make the next assault. Tyler's brigade formed with the 129th Pennsylvania on the left of the front line, with the 134th Pennsylvania on the right. The second line had the 91st Pennsylvania on the left and the 126th Pennsylvania on the right.[88] The sun was beginning to set as the men in the brigade made their final preparations for the advance.[89] Once the preparations were complete, General Humphreys told the men: "Boys, you are ordered to take that stone wall, and must do it with the bayonet."[90] The men cheered as the bugles blared the command to charge.

The line advanced splendidly. Not a single shot was fired "until the advance was within three or four rods" of the men of Allabach's brigade. General Tyler, leading the brigade, was waving his sword and "encouraging his men by voice and example." But "[s]uddenly a wall of flaming fire, shot and shell struck Tyler's Brigade." The firing from the wall caused a tremendous volume of smoke which temporarily obstructed the vision of the observers. When the mist lifted, "Tyler's Brigade had vanished as completely as if they had been swallowed."[91] All that remained was a "windrow of dead."[92] An effort was made to reform the line, but "the increased darkness prevented the marshaling of the thinned ranks."[93] The men, already tired after a long day on the field, lay down with their comrades to hide and rest from their ordeal.

The end result of this assault was the same as all of the others. Hundreds of new casualties dotted the hill leading up to the stone wall. But thankfully for the division and the army, this was the last assault attempted on the heights. Night was now enveloping the field and the men in the brigade slowly retired from the front. The Battle of Fredericksburg was over, but the men did not leave the field despondent. General Humphreys brought the troops to the ravine with "the One Hundred and twenty-third and the One Hundred and Fifty-fifth Regiments, commanded by Colonels Clark and Allen, retiring slowly and in good order, singing and hurrahing."[94] Colonel Allabach brought off the "right wing . . . the men in the mean time cheering."[95]

The men retreated to the safety of the ravine where the ill-fated assault began. Night had fallen on the field and it was difficult, if not impossible, to distinguish friend from foe. Most of the regiments, in retreating to the ravine, had forsaken all semblance of formation. To make matters worse, a thick fog enveloped the field and severely reduced visibility.

The difficulties experienced in the retreat were not merely confined to the individual members of the brigade. Due to the lateness of the assault and the darkness that now covered the field, Colonel Allabach had no idea where each of his regiments was located. The situation was further exacerbated by the heavy fog. This confusion caused the members of the 123rd and the 155th to spend a long night on the field.

After the attack, the men from both units quickly sought shelter in and around the ravine. They stayed at this location believing that they had been ordered to stay on the battlefield. Late in the evening, however, the commanders of both units realized that the rest of the brigade had left the field to go into town. As a result, Colonel Allen, the commander of the 155th, sent a number of his men into the fog in hopes of finding General Humphreys. But the fog was so dense "that hours passed by" with no word from the dispatched men. These couriers later reported that they "could not find either the [missing] regiments or the town of Fredericksburg."[96] Colonel Allen finally made the trip himself and luckily found General Humphreys' headquarters. He related that both the 123rd and the 155th had been overlooked and were in need of orders. Only then were the regiments directed to march into town and join the rest of the brigade.[97]

Upon entering the town, the two lost regiments were furnished with more ammunition and marched back to their former position where they remained until daylight. The sounds that emanated from the field would long be remembered by the men. A member of the brigade recalled: "The cries of the wounded rose over the bloody field like the wail of lost spirits, all the night the 'cries for water, blankets and to be borne off the field', in all the paroxisms that terror and suffering can excite, went up from the sad victims of the days' havoc and filled the air with pain."[98]

A soldier from the 123rd, who was clearly haunted by the memory of his night on the field, attempted to capture his feelings in a poem written shortly after his discharge:

> The night came on—oh fearful night
> Yet blessed night, for all—
> God's sheltering roof, o'er living men,
> O'er dead His funeral pall;
> Some slept as weary soldiers sleep,
> But gasping by my side,
> Poor Harry lay, in chills of death,
> Ere morning broke—he died.
>
> "Now John, you're going home," said he
> "And tell my mother this"
> "Forget my faults, forgive me all"
> "I've ever done amiss;"

"My battle's o'er, I loved the Flag,"
"Next to my God and her,"
"And dying in my country's cause,"
"Tis I am conqueror."

"And tell her not to grieve for me"
"We'll meet again in Heaven,"
"For Jesus' blood was shed I know,"
"That I might be forgiven."
And then he prayed—and soon was still,
I knew that he was dead,
Yet laid me down beside the corpse,
And slept as in a bed.[99]

The suffering of the men was compounded by a cold December night. Many of the soldiers had taken off their overcoats and blankets prior to the charge. These men were forced to lay on the cold ground and seek whatever warmth they could find. Some huddled close to the dead for warmth. Others stayed close to the wounded for heat. Some even stripped clothing from the dead as protection from the cold December wind. Lieutenant Alexander Carson of the 155th remembered that the "sights and sounds" of the 14th were never "equaled in any later battle during the war."[100]

The regiment stayed on the field until 8 P.M. on Sunday, December 14. As soon as the Sabbath dawned, "firing commenced between the pickets, and continued all day." The men were exposed to the rebel sharpshooters on the hill above and to the shells of a battery on the right flank. This combination of fire forced the men "to lie low all . . . day on mud mingled with the ruins of knapsacks, with here and there a dead man lying unburied." About eight o'clock the regiment was relieved and placed in battle line on Main Street.[101]

The 14th also brought home, firsthand, the horrors of war. While the men had endured the myriad of sounds during the night of the 13th, the dawn revealed the visual aspects of the battle's aftermath. Ambulances were passing all day through the streets of the city. Hundreds of wounded men could be seen with blood streaming down their faces. Sergeant Brackenridge of the

123rd passed a hospital tent and saw "eight dead bodies in front of it and at least twenty amputated arms and legs."[102]

The dead from the previous day's carnage could be seen lying everywhere. A member of the 24th New Jersey described a dead soldier he encountered: "I continued my course down the hill until I reached the open field where I stopped at the ruins of a small brick house, destroyed by shells. Inside the walls a dead soldier laid on a heap of crumbled bricks . . . Upon the breast of the lifeless body lay a prettily bound volume of 'The Book of Common Prayer.'"[103] In all likelihood, the dead soldier belonged to the 123rd. It will be remembered that Thomas Howe, the benefactor of Company C, gave each member of his company a copy of this book prior to their departure. In his presentation speech, he earnestly prayed that this small token would offer "guidance and protection" to the men of this unit and bring each safely home. Sadly for this one soldier, the prayers of Mr. Howe would not be answered. This lone soldier would never find his way home to his loved ones in Pittsburgh.

But many of the other wounded combatants were still alive and in need of medical care. Due to the sheer number of casualties, the treatment provided by the divisional hospitals was both sporadic and inadequate. Chaplain Hartsock spent December 13 through December 15 visiting many of the divisional hospitals. The sights he witnessed left a lasting impression:

> The scenes in the hospital of amputations, probing, cutting, drawing bullets, setting limbs &c will forever be impressed upon my mind . . . After night by some means I went to a large two story church. I had a lantern, tho it was dangerous business to carry a light when the enemy pointed his guns to it . . . When I entered the church I found it full of wounded and as I entered I was hailed by name from voices, 'Chaplain see here I am dying for want of attention,' 'Give me a drink,' 'Get me a surgeon to dress my wounds' and many such pleadings . . . I at once went for candles, and got men to come with water. Brought some surgeons. When we entered the pale faces of the dead, with their sightless eyes, stared upon us. Ah! what a scene of suffering.[104]

As was the custom, the army began the gruesome task of burying its dead immediately following the battle. On the evening of the 13th and throughout the day on the 14th, the men attempted to complete this task. Although the soldiers worked diligently, the crews lacked the necessary equipment to properly care for the slain. Men were sent out to carry in the wounded and the dead, but there were few stretchers. Priority was given to the living, and most of the wounded were brought into town by dawn.

Private Dallas' Grave in Pittsburgh
Photograph by Author

Many of the slain were still on the field at sunrise. The following night, burying parties were sent out, but "it was extremely difficult to distinguish ours, and utterly impossible for the parties to bring off all who were laying there. The bodies of many of the men were, therefore, left there."[105]

Colonel Clark mentioned three of the slain men of the 123rd in his letter of December 18:

> Of the several killed, we only got one buried before we retired across the river. The body of Alexander Dallas, of company E, was buried near where we fought, and the spot marked with a board having his name upon it. The body of Lieut. Coulter was left in the hospital unburied, as was also Sergeant Kipp, of company F. The comrades of Kipp attempted his burial, but were not allowed even that sad pleasure, by rebel sharpshooters.[106]

Alexander Dallas did not remain on the fields of Fredericksburg for long. His body was disinterred and sent home to Allegheny for a proper burial in Union Dale Cemetery. His grave is marked with a headstone which commemorates his ultimate sacrifice on the field at Fredericksburg.

On the morning of December 15, the division received orders to send all the wounded back across the river. Chaplain Hartsock of the 133rd and Chaplain H. L. Chapman of the 123rd accompanied the men. All who could walk were sent across the pontoons first. The moving was "very hard on the men," with "many moans and . . . sharp pains."[107]

The new hospital was set up near the Phillips House. Late in the evening, the wounded, except for those who could not be moved, were sent to Washington. After all had been sent, the chaplains of both regiments had supper and lay down to rest.[108]

The other members of the regiment remained in the city for the balance of their time on the southern banks of the Rappahannock. Private Borland recorded on the 15th that the men "remained in the town under cover of the houses all day; there was considerable shelling by the rebs, but few casualties—none at all in our regiment."[109] Private Ross remembered that the regiment "la[y] on the sidewalk for the night."[110]

At about 9 P.M. on the 15th, the regiment received orders to prepare for the retreat across the Rappahannock. Humphreys' Division was designated as the rear guard and assigned to cover Burnside's retreat. Corporal Rhein recalled that this "honor" ultimately caused the division some problems: ". . . [W]e were ordered to fall back quietly and march for the pontoons, so we knew we were on retreat. As we went out at one end of the town, the Johnnies came in at the other and gobbled up a good many of our men who had quartered themselves in houses in order to make themselves more comfortable. It was their own fault as they should have been with their companies and regiments."[111]

The orders issued to the men were emphatic. No one was to "speak above a whisper nor to let their tins jingle as to inform the enemy of [their] intentions . . ."[112] The men of the 123rd "religiously" followed these orders. They quietly waited their turn on the southern side of the Rappahannock until approximately 2 A.M. when they received their orders to cross. Similar to the beginning of the campaign, it began to rain during the crossing. Colonel Clark remembered that "it began to rain, and all the way back to our old camp, some four miles, it poured down upon us till our clothing was pretty saturated. Many were so exhausted by former fatigue and by wading in the mud, that they were forced to lay down and rest. But before the setting of the sun, nearly every man reported himself in camp."[113] Private Borland placed their time of arrival at camp at about 11 A.M.; the rain ceasing about the time they arrived. He wrote in his diary: "we arrived about 11 A.M., entirely satisfied with our experience in war."[114]

The Fredericksburg campaign was now over; all that remained was the tallying of the army's losses and the debate over who was responsible for the defeat. But nowhere in the debate was the courage and heart of Humphreys' Division ever questioned. The men had "seen the elephant" and had passed their first test in battle with flying colors.

General Hooker paid the division its highest honor during his testimony before the Committee on the Conduct of the War on December 20, 1862. On that day, he passionately stated: "There never was anything more glorious than the behavior of the men. No campaign in the world ever saw a more gallant advance than Humphreys' division made there. But they were put to do work that no men could do."[115]

CHAPTER FOUR
THE AFTERMATH OF FREDERICKSBURG

I have fought a good fight, I have finished my course, I have kept the faith.

2 Timothy 4:7
Text of Colonel Clark's sermon to the regiment for January 18, 1863

The battle of Fredericksburg was the most important engagement for the men of the 123rd. In the days, weeks, and even months after the battle, much was written by the Northern populace regarding the contest. The local residents of Allegheny and Pittsburgh fearfully awaited the accounts to learn of the fate of their loved ones. Initially, all news reports described the bravery of the participants. Soon, the accounts became more personal as the sterile casualty numbers bore names. But as the days moved on, questions arose regarding the strategy and leadership in the Union ranks. The bravery of the participants slowly gave way to the question, "What went wrong?" As the months and years passed, and the Union won more complimentary battles, this battle began to fade in the collective memories of the people in the North. The stories of the participants helped to keep the memory alive for some time as debates raged over which regiment got closer to the wall, or which unit was the bravest. Many of the debates were friendly disputes among comrades, while others were far more contentious. But as the participants died, so too did the tales of these courageous men. As the decades moved on, the charge up Marye's Heights soon was relegated to a footnote in many of the Civil War writings.

After the battle, the first order of business was to tally the losses. The casualty figures reported by the regiments in Humphreys' Division were staggering. The losses were summarized in Humphreys' after-battle report. Even worse than the losses was the realization that the casualties had been in vain. Christian Rhein of Company B sarcastically wrote: "We did not accomplish much in the battle except to leave behind us a lot of killed and wounded men."[1] Colonel Clark did not criticize his superiors for their roles in the loss; he only noted, ". . . lest I offend, I will give no opinion in regard to the propriety and results in the battle, nor yet of its management."[2]

General Hooker was not as tactful. When asked why he had suspended the attacks, Hooker initially replied: "Finding that I had lost as many men as my orders required me to lose, I suspended the attack, and directed that the men should hold . . ." When pressed further as to the effectiveness of the attack on the stone wall, he only responded that it had been no more effective than what you "could make upon the side of a mountain of rock."[3]

The participants of the charge debated for years how close the army came to the wall. Along with this discussion came the question of which unit reached the farthest point in the attack. Many units stepped forward to stake their claim and argue their case. The most acrimonious participants in this debate were General Humphreys' son, Lieutenant Colonel Henry H. Humphreys, and the historian of the II Corps, General Francis A. Walker.[4]

The dispute began in 1886 when General Walker published a book about the feats of the II Corps. Unfortunately, in his book he commented about the exploits of Humphreys' Division. He denied that the men of the II Corps obstructed Humphreys Division's path to the wall and wrote:

> It is very likely that among the thousands a few may have called out to Allabach's and Tyler's men that it was useless to go forward, but their own situation on that field swept by fire, is proof that such men were few, if indeed, the story is not the tale of some colonel or captain to excuse the breaking of his command.[5]

The general further contended that the men of the II Corps got closer to the wall than the men from Humphreys' Division. He cited a number of specific instances that helped to bolster his position. Both comments were read by Colonel Humphreys, who felt honor bound to defend the reputation of his father and the division.

Letters between the two were exchanged for the next four years with charges and countercharges made by each. General Walker agreed in the early part of the debate to delete the last 21 words in the above paragraph to appease Colonel Humphreys. But he never budged from his position that the men of the II Corps got closest to the wall. He wrote the colonel in January of 1889:

> Neither General Humphreys or yourself nor any officer or soldier of the division, so far as it appears by the records, witnessed any one of the charges made by the 2d Corps against the wall. On the other hand, thousands of officers and men witnessed alike the charges of Humphreys' Division and those made by the divisions of French, Hancock and Howard. I have yet to learn of a single person who enjoyed those opportunities who holds with you.[6]

At the end of the letter, the general offered his antagonist the following fatherly advice: "This is all I have to say on the subject. If your mind is not satisfied, I do not see but what we shall have to agree to disagree regarding the matter as men have to do respecting many points, in this and every other war in human history . . . Whatever may be written, I, for one, entertain no fear that any intelligent and disinterested American will believe the divisions of French, Hancock and Howard to have been inferior in courage, discipline and efficiency to the gallant regiments that composed the brigades of Allabach and Tyler."[7]

The advice offered by General Walker did little to dissuade Colonel Humphreys from further pursuing his claims. While he waited almost 13 months to pen his final response to the general, he did make one last attempt to sway his adversary. The letter sent in April of 1890 contained no new revelations regarding the controversy. The colonel quoted extensively from many of the reports from the recently published *Official Records*, but these handpicked documents, like General Walker's, only presented the viewpoint of Colonel Humphreys and offered little help in resolving the dispute.

In the letter's last paragraph, Colonel Humphreys summarized his reasons for writing his final response: "[W]ere General Humphreys living, he would have pointed out wherein you were wrong, and on his statements you would have corrected the errors committed. Due regard for those whose lips are sealed in death, coupled with admiration for the green division, has called forth this letter."[8]

But General Walker, true to his word, never answered the colonel's April letter. The correspondence between the two antagonists ceased without any clearcut winner. But for the men of both divisions, the dispute never ended.

In the latter part of 1891, another salvo was fired by the men of Humphreys' Division. At that time, Robert Fleming, an officer in the Richmond Fayette Artillery, wrote a highly publicized letter about the aftermath of the charge. For many, this was the most conclusive evidence to date to support the division's position that they came closest to the wall. The letter stated:

> A day after the battle I went out with the flag of truce between the lines to see about burying the dead, but more especially to find the body of Captain King, who was on General McLaws' Staff, and was killed during the assault. I saw the dead as they had fallen in these charges, and while I do not wish to detract from the hard fought but bloody battle in which they were repulsed, yet I must in justice say that the bodies that I saw close to the works belonged to General Humphreys' Division.[9]

While there is no recorded response by the II Corps to the above statement, it is highly unlikely that the members of this unit were swayed by Lieutenant Fleming's letter. Suffice it to say that the members of each unit went to their graves steadfastly defending the honor of their comrades. And like General Walker once told Colonel Humphreys, they had to agree to disagree. Such is the nature of war.

But the dispute regarding the proximity to the wall was not only confined to the divisions of Humphreys and Hancock. The controversy also spilled over into the regimental ranks. The debate, however, was much quieter and never approached the testiness of the quarrel between Humphreys and Walker. Two regiments, nonetheless, would present their claims that their unit came closest to the wall. Both units were members of Allabach's brigade.

The first regiment to claim this honor was the 131st Pennsylvania.[10] The men cited as authority for their argument the statements of Martha Stephens, the individual who owned the house just in front of the Confederate line. Mrs. Stephens had testified, shortly after the battle, that on the night of the 13th, "all the clothes had been stripped from the bodies of the Union soldiers" who lay in close proximity to her house. She recalled that at the farthest point reached in the charge were "three soldier caps, bearing the numbers 131 P.V."[11] As a result, the men of the 131st argued that they had reached the farthest point in the advance.

The 155th took exception to the assertions made by the 131st. While the members of the regiment never directly assailed the statements of their brigade comrades, they did contend, in their regimental history, that their unit came closest to the wall.[12] The men told the story of one of their regiments, on the day after the battle, being detailed to recover the dead and the wounded of the unit. This individual found Private Philip Linderman of Company D "lying closer to the famous stonewall than that of any other soldier on that portion of Marye's Heights."[13]

How close any of these men or units came to the wall is clearly open to some question. Many estimates have been offered regarding each unit's proximity to the wall. Colonel Allabach contended that his brigade was "within 12 paces of the stone wall."[14] General Hooker placed "[t]he head of General Humphreys column . . . perhaps fifteen to twenty yards from the stone wall."[15]

But by far, the majority of the participants remembered that the nearest they came to the wall was about 50 yards. Colonel Clark noted that "[w]here we fought they were fifty yards off, behind a stone wall."[16] Colonel Speakman of the 133rd and Colonel Allen of the 155th also placed the battle line within 50 yards of the stone wall.[17]

But no matter how close they came, the praise the division received in the succeeding days and months after the battle was universal. General Humphreys told the men in January that "his only wish was that the nine months [term] was for nine years instead of nine months."[18] In *Harper's Weekly*, the "gallant charge" of Humphreys' Division was specifically mentioned with glowing accolades. In the weeks after the battle, the newspaper reported that "[o]lder soldiers than they quailed before the murderous volleys."[19] *Harper's Weekly* was the first to publicly refer to Humphreys' charge as the "forlorn hope." The men took great pride in this name. Considering the newness of the troops, this pride was clearly understandable. As one member of the division later observed: "That General Humphreys command should be chosen as the 'forlorn hope' by fighting Joe Hooker was bestowing on it no trivial honor . . ."[20] The Pittsburgh papers also spoke proudly of the achievements of the 123rd. In an article published in the *Pittsburgh Dispatch* on December 27, the editor noted: "The 155th . . . [and the]123d, . . . officers and men, sustained the reputation of the Old Keystone. If fault is found to Pennsylvania, it cannot be laid at their doors."[21]

But by far, the most complimentary commentary on the charge was by an unnamed Confederate soldier in the *Confederate Veteran*. He wrote:

> When we left the wall the gallant Federals in five lines of battle were on the charge. I have since learned this was Humphreys Division of Hooker's Reserves . . . Confederates might have made a more impetuous charge, but for cool persistent courage there is no instance in the whole history of the war that surpasses this charge of Humphreys.[22]

The men and officers of the division were also proud of their achievements. General Humphreys was no exception. While it is not often spoken of, it must be remembered that General Humphreys was 52 years old at the time of the battle and had never had a field command. Although it is true that he had been in the military for many years, most of his time had been spent in the topographic department. While there is little question that General Humphreys would never admit any doubts about his abilities, he surely must have had some concerns regarding his own proficiency in battle. All would agree that he passed his initial test with high marks.

But more important to General Humphreys was his own realization that he was an effective battlefield commander. He recorded in a December 17 letter his feelings at the time of the assault:

> For a moment the thought passed through my mind that it was a strange scene for father and son to pass through. The charge of my division is described by those who witnessed it as sublime, and Henry tells me that he heard some general officers who saw it (who did not know me) discussing it, and saying, that it was the grandest sight they ever saw, and that as I led the charge and bared my head, raising my right arm to heaven, the setting sun shining full upon my face gave me the aspect of an inspired being. This is quite egotistical, is it not? I felt gloriously . . .[23]

He later wrote to a friend named Campbell his further thoughts about the battle: "Campbell, I felt like a young girl of sixteen at her first ball; I felt more like a god than a man; I now understand what Charles XII meant when he said, 'Let the whistling of the bullets hereafter be my music.'"[24]

But for many of the men and officers of the regiment the battle was not as romantic as General Humphreys portrayed. Colonel Clark, unlike his commander, only saw the suffering the battle caused his men and their families. He touchingly wrote:

> I have thus far desisted from any mention of the disasters resulting from the battle. This to me is too sad a task. At the earliest moment possible, I obtained a list of the killed and wounded, forwarding it for publication. That list, I have since learned was pretty accurate . . . I hope that ere this, it has been published for the information of anxious friends. How

their hearts must bleed. Oh! God pity the bereaved—the soldier's widow and fatherless children! Let heaven's healing balm, soothe and heal every heart wrung with pain, and broken with anxiety. To know the fact that your friends fought bravely and shed their life's blood to perpetuate liberty in the land, is an honor that will never perish. But it won't replace the dear lost ones, nor make their homes ring with joy, like the return and presence of those you so much loved. Jesus only can comfort in an hour like this. He can only heal the broken heart and turn your sadness into gladness.[25]

For the men in the ranks, few, if any, saw the battle in a positive light. Most were just glad that the ordeal was over and they had survived. Sergeant L. Brakenridge, speaking for many in the regiment, wondered: "How I escaped—how I arrived safe, is a miracle."[26] Private Borland noted in his diary, ". . . now that the battle is over I must say that the horrors of battle to be realized must be seen."[27]

Many spoke highly of their fellow comrades. Lieutenant Samuel D. Karns of Company I told the constituents of Pittsburgh and Allegheny of the courage of their leader. The lieutenant wrote: "Col. Clark, exhibited the utmost coolness and bravery . . . [T]he boys liked him before, but they like him <u>better</u> now. He is every inch a soldier."[28]

Colonel John P. Glass from Pittsburgh witnessed Humphreys' charge and told the people of Allegheny and Pittsburgh that "never did men acquit themselves so handsomely. They were cool as veterans even under the heaviest of fire and displayed gallantry throughout. " He personally saw Colonel Clark and Colonel Allen (commander of the 155th) being "publicly complimented by General Humphreys after the battle."[29]

The praise of Colonel Clark was not only confined to local sources. General Humphreys, the somewhat stoic leader of the division, mirrored both individuals' assessment of the local minister. A member of the brigade told of the general's feelings regarding the colonel:

Colonel Clark, the commander of the One Hundred and Twenty-third, was a brave soldier, who received from the dashing General Humphreys, the Division commander, the great compliment on the battlefield of Fredericksburg, where the regiment participated in the bloody charge on Marye's Heights, that "after all, the Preacher-Colonel would fight." The earnest and intense language used by the Division General in compliment to Reverend Colonel Clark was emphasized with profanity, which the Reverend Colonel, under other circumstances, would undoubtedly have reproved.[30]

Colonel Clark was equally as complimentary of the men in the regiment. He would write in his report: "I am glad to say that very few of my men exhibited cowardice."[31] In a letter after the battle, the colonel, after telling of his own personal experience, noted: "The nearest I came to a wound was the sting of a ball on my cheek. The sensation soon passed . . . Our fight was the hottest of the day. My men, indeed the whole brigade, behaved well."[32]

General Humphreys placed the regiment's losses at 15 killed, 106 wounded, and 13 missing.[33] In Colonel Clark's initial report he listed 16 killed, 115 wounded, and 97 missing.[34] In Bates' compilation for the Pennsylvania legislature, he only recorded 26 killed, 29 wounded, and 10 missing.[35] Since Bates has been known to sometimes underreport the number of casualties, the numbers given by Humphreys and the *Gazette* better represents the proper casualty figures.

In the entire army, the losses by Humphreys' Division, and more specifically by Allabach's brigade, put both units in the upper ranks of casualties. Humphreys' losses ranked fifth among divisions that participated in the battle. Two of the divisions above Humphreys', Meade's and Gibbon's, were involved in the battle on the left of the line. As a result, Humphreys' Division ranked third among divisions that participated in the assault on Marye's Heights.[36]

Allabach's casualties ranked even higher among the brigades. The unit which contained the 123rd ranked fifth among all brigades for losses in the battle. Three of the brigades with higher losses had been engaged on the left of the line. Only Caldwell's brigade of Hancock's Division had higher losses in the assault on the heights.[37]

When Humphreys' divisional losses are added to the other casualties in the army, the number totals 12,653. Of this number, over one-half, or 7,348, were lost in the many ill-fated charges up Marye's Heights.[38]

In comparison, the casualty figures for Pickett's Charge were recorded as 6,467.[39] In contrasting these number with the losses experienced during the attack at Fredericksburg, it is clear that a comparable number of men were lost during each charge. In truth, more men were lost during the charges at Fredericksburg than at the attack on Cemetery Ridge. Yet the latter has received more exposure than the former. Why then has this charge been forgotten?

The answer may lie in a number of different areas. Initially, one must look at the nature of each event to see where part of the difference lies. The charge on Marye's Heights was a number of disjointed actions which culminated in relatively the same location. There was not a grand charge with a large number of men moving in unison across an open field.[40] Quite the contrary, there were at least seven distinct attacks that moved up the hill at different times throughout the day.

Further, while the numerical losses during both charges were relatively the same, during Pickett's Charge, the percentage of losses in each division was clearly higher. Many units lost over 50 percent of their men during the attack. Some lost over 75 percent. While Humphreys would lose close to 25 percent and Hancock close to 50 percent, no division approached Pickett's percentage of losses.

For short-term units, like the 123rd, one might expect that many of the men would write about their most important battle. But that never happened. For many members, who were older with families, getting back to normal life was far more important than extolling their accomplishments. Some joined other regiments which participated in later, more successful battles. While many wrote of the attack, no one ever stepped forward to glorify the attack or the men who made the charge.

In truth, the charge at Fredericksburg actually became the antithesis of Pickett's Charge. Rather than becoming a symbol of heroism and glory, the attack became a symbol of the incompetence of the Northern army during its first two years at war. If the charge was spoken of at all, it was couched in such terms as "ill-fated" or "disastrous." Most individuals were willing to forget this battle and discuss the Northern successes at Gettysburg, Petersburg, and ultimately Appomattox. Few wanted to talk about a battle that left so many of their brethren dead in a totally useless attack.

The men who made this charge were lost in this Northern embarrassment. Many, similar to the men of the 123rd, had never been in battle before. They watched as regiment after regiment was sent up the hill, only to see the scattered remnants of these units lying dead and mutilated when the smoke cleared. These men, like the men in Pickett's attack, did what they were told to do; without any thought or concern for their safety. It is this forgotten aspect of the battle that is most unfortunate. Both groups deserve their due, but to the men at Fredericksburg, their due has never come.

To the families in Allegheny and Pittsburgh, the heroism of their residents was not foremost in their minds after the battle. Most had a relative or someone they knew who had participated in the attack. These individuals waited anxiously for news from the battlefield. It took some time for any reports to filter back to Allegheny County. The first accounts initially reported that the regiment was not even engaged in the battle. This information, which reported that the unit was on the northern side of the Rappahannock at 11:00 A.M., was correct, as far as it went.[41] At that time, the regiment was, in fact, not on the combative side of the Rappahannock. But shortly thereafter, the regiment did cross the river and proceed to the battlefield.

On December 19, the *Pittsburgh Gazette* removed all doubt of the regiment's fate. At that time, the paper published a list of the known killed and wounded under the heading: "List of Casualties in Col. Clark's Regiment—16 Killed, 115 wounded and 97 Missing."[42] The local constituency could no longer cling to the hope that their friends and family members had been spared. For some, this may have been their first notification that a friend or loved one had been lost.

For the wife, child, and friends of Captain Daniel Boisol, their worst fears were realized. The 39-year-old dentist, who left a lucrative practice in August 1862 to lead his company, was dying from the wounds he received during the charge. A letter written on December 15 from a member of the 155th noted: "Dr. Boisol, Captain of a company in Clark's Regiment, is, I am afraid, fatally wounded. He was shot in the groin by a musket or rifle ball, and his bladder is severed."[43]

Captain Boisol died of his wounds on December 28 at 11 P.M. at College Hospital in Washington. His body was returned to Allegheny and his funeral conducted at his residence on Robinson Street on January 2, 1863.

The men of Company G penned a fitting epitaph to their fallen captain. They sadly recorded:

> In our late commander we feel that we have lost a friend. Though a strict disciplinarian, and requiring a faithful performance of duty on the part of the men, he was ever watchful of their comfort, kind to the sick, and anxious for the good of his whole company. Ever ready for duty, which he always faithfully performed; brave and cool in battle, in him the service has lost an intelligent, intrepid and energetic officer . . . We trust that God of the Armies and Battles has only said to him "Come up higher." We believe that he had taken Christ to be the Captain of salvation, and that our loss is his eternal gain.[44]

The loss of their beloved captain and comrades was a difficult time for the regiment. It was a low point for all of the men. The poet of the regiment summed up their feelings best when he wrote:

> A bloody fight, two sleepless nights—
> And days, in mire and rain,
> Ten Thousand brave men fell behind,
> Sums up the dark campaign.[45]

Daniel Boisol
Dentist and captain of Company G. He was wounded in the assault and died on December 28, 1862.

Under the Maltese Cross

Captain Boisol's weathered gravestone in Union Dale Cemetery in Pittsburgh.
Photograph by Author

CHAPTER FIVE
REST, RECUPERATION, AND THE MUD MARCH

O thou sword of the Lord, how long will it be ere thou be quiet? Put up thyself into thy scabbard, rest and be still.
Jeremiah 47:6–7
Text of Colonel Clark's sermon for August 10, 1862

Upon their arrival in camp on December 16, the men of the 123rd spent the remainder of the day resting from their ordeal. The regiment established camp in close proximity to the area it occupied prior to its march to the battlefield. Both Privates Ross and Borland commented on the solitude in camp.[1]

For many, the loneliness in camp was due, in part, to the sudden realization of the severity of the division's losses. Chaplain Hartsock of the 133rd explained: "I feel sad as I entered the old camp. I could not help thinking of the comrades and friends who left camp with us, who now lie either in their shallow graves or on beds of suffering in the various hospitals. There are many messes broken up, many tents vacant, many wooden chimneys send forth no smoke, how small our number seems."[2]

The men began to realize that in all likelihood, they would spend the winter in camp. Lieutenant Brackenridge noted in a December 21 letter that "[w]e have been ordered to enlarge our camp, and to make ourselves as comfortable as possible."[3]

During the latter part of December, the regiment was also in desperate need of food, clothing, and medicine. The majority of the men in the regiment had lost their knapsacks after the battle at Fredericksburg.[4] Colonel Clark was clearly concerned about this and noted his apprehensions in a letter dated December 24:

99

Hospital supplies were considerably exhausted during the days of the engagement, but that Christian gentleman, Mr. Brunot, who is ever looking after the interests of the soldiers, brought us a timely addition to our stock, which will make our men comfortable for a few days. Other friends I know would send us supplies, but, for some reason, express goods are regarded at Washington, as almost contraband of war. There have been, I may say, scores of boxes there for the men for some time, but my order would not bring them, and our superiors would not allow any one to be sent for them. Unless there is a speedy change, I fear the men will be short of the luxuries during the holidays.[5]

Colonel Clark's fears were well founded. The regiment did not receive their much-needed supplies by Christmas Day, but they did not seem to mind the mixup. Many dressed in their best uniforms and visited other members of the division. Others spent their time writing to loved ones—undoubtedly about the great battle they participated in.

The much-needed supplies finally reached the regiment on New Year's Day. Their arrival made the New Year's festivities much more upbeat than the Christmas frivolities. A correspondent for the *Gazette* reported on January 1: "The boys are indulging their epicurean desires by regaling on the good things sent from home . . . Christmas was rather dull, but New Years has been enlivened with turkeys, etc."[6]

While many used this time for merriment, others reflected on their own situations and those of the country. Private Borland noted his thoughts about the past year and his hopes for the future:

Another eventful year has passed, one which will ever be remembered in our country's history, during all its long days the rebellion has been raging from one end of our land to the other with varied success, and it does seem to me to appear much nearer a close than at its commencement. May the present year chronicle the downfall of the rebellion and with it every system of oppression and iniquity through our land.[7]

During the latter part of December and early January, the regiment experienced a further reduction in its ranks. Four more men died from illness during this period: Gottlieb Burkhart of Company B (December 28, 1862), William Caldwell of Company A (January 2, 1863), and William Edwards of Company I (January 4, 1863) died in the division's field hospital at Falmouth; William Cowley of Company E was sent to Aquia Creek for treatment and perished on December 19, 1862. While there is no question that the doctors in the division did all that they could for the sick, in reality appropriate medical treatment was not available. This substandard care prompted one soldier to write: "[The] hospital was a good place to die, but a very poor place to get well."[8]

All four of the men were buried in graves located very close to their place of death. After the war their remains were disinterred and buried in other locations. Two of the aforementioned individuals, William Caldwell and William Edwards, were reburied in the Fredericksburg National Cemetery. The final resting places of the two other soldiers are not known.

The ranks were also further reduced by medical discharges. During the 123rd's nine months in the field, no other period of time had more members discharged than during this stretch. Whether the rigors of the recent battle caused the rash of illnesses was never indicated by any of the men. But some of the men did have their own theories on the reasons for these discharges. Private Hemphill theorized that many of the men's "patriotism [was] 'played out' as the boys here say."[9] Whatever the true reasons were for the departures, 14 men from the regiment were discharged between December 20, 1862, and January 20, 1863.[10]

The most significant loss, however, came from the ranks of the regimental commanders. On December 31, 1862, Captain Henry Maxwell of Company K resigned his commission. While no evidence has been found explaining the reasons for Captain Maxwell's resignation, it came too late to save his health. On September 27, 1865, the former commander of Company K died at the age of 39. He was buried in Union Dale Cemetery near his fellow comrade and fallen friend, Daniel Boisol.

Henry Maxwell
Captain Maxwell, *second from the left*, with a pipe, resigned
from the regiment on December 31, 1862.

USAMHI—Tibbals Collection

The weathered grave of Captain Maxwell in the
Union Dale Cemetery.

Photograph by Author

With the exception of typical military duties, life at the regimental level in the weeks following the battle was monotonous, but this was not the case within the Union high command. In the days and weeks after the battle, many Union officers and governmental officials had withheld their opinions concerning who was responsible for the Fredericksburg debacle. This began to change during the latter part of December and early part of January, as many began to clamor for some accountability.

In truth, no one was really sure who was at fault for the defeat at Fredericksburg. This growing frustration caused many to question the war effort. An article that appeared in the December 27, 1862, *Harper's Weekly* dramatically explained the attitudes displayed by many Northerners:

> We are indulging in no hyperbole when we say that these events are rapidly filling the heart[s] of the loyal North with sickness, disgust, and despair. Party lines are becoming effaced by such unequivocal evidences of administrative imbecility; it is the men who have given and trusted the most, and now feel keenly that the Government is unfit for its office, and that the most gallant efforts ever made by a cruelly tried people are being neutralized by the obstinacy and incapacity of their leaders. Where this will end no one can see. But it must end soon. The people have shown patience, during this past year, quite unexampled in history. They have borne, silently and grimly, imbecility, treachery, failure, privation, loss of friends and means, almost every suffering which can afflict a brave people. But they can not be expected to suffer that such massacres as this at Fredericksburg shall be repeated. Matters are rapidly ripening for a military dictatorship.[11]

Many Union generals seriously questioned Burnside's ability to command. Brigadier Generals John Cochrane and John Newton made a special trip to Washington to express their concerns to the president. Both were mere brigade commanders who had obviously forgotten the military protocol related to the chain of command. Nonetheless, Lincoln met with these individuals on December 30 and agreed with their assessment of the situation.[12]

At the meeting, the generals informed the president of Burnside's plan to cross the Rappahannock in hopes of outflanking the Confederate positions. Both vehemently told the president that the army had lost confidence in their commander and that any form of movement would meet with disaster. General Cochrane explained, "Mr. President, to have withheld from you these facts, I should not have ranked at any criminal grade below treason." Lincoln, not knowing who or what to believe, instructed Burnside to postpone the maneuver until he could discuss the matter further with General Halleck and Secretary Stanton.[13]

Burnside sensed the growing displeasure among his subordinates. On December 31, he offered his resignation to the president, but Lincoln refused to accept. The president only stated: "I do not yet see how I could profit by changing the command of the A. P. [Army of the Potomac] . . ."[14] This gesture of good faith, for the time being, seemed to provide a momentary reprieve to General Burnside's floundering command.

In the early weeks of January, Burnside began to formulate a new strategy of attack using the upstream fords of the Rappahannock. His final plan proposed that the majority of the army would cross at Banks' Ford, while two smaller forces would feint crossings at United States Ford and Muddy Creek.[15] According to Burnside, this plan would force Lee's army out of their entrenchments and into the open where the Union army could fight them on equal terms. Although not totally convinced of the scheme's merits, Lincoln endorsed the proposal, but cautioned Burnside that the country did not want rash action.

On January 18, individual orders were sent to each command to commence the march the next day. Burnside's infamous "Mud March" was about to begin. The movement was doomed from the start, as the roads were not in the best of shape when the march began.

On January 16, heavy rain fell during the early morning. The 17th was cold and caused a heavy freeze, and on the 18th, the

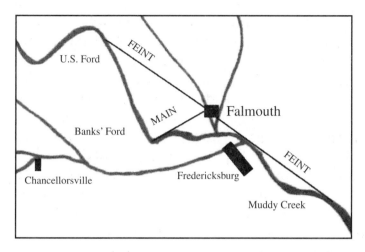

Burnside's Mud March

ground was again frozen solid, which postponed the march for 24 hours.[16] On the 19th the weather was very cold and the ground was still frozen, which caused the marching orders to be countermanded for another 24 hours.

At one o'clock in the afternoon on January 20, the infantrymen were ordered to strike their tents and begin the march. The men stood under arms until 4 P.M. when the advance began. They traveled about two miles and came to rest for the night in a beautiful pine grove. At about 8 P.M., it began to rain and continued throughout the night. Private Borland described the evening and the early morning hours: "It commenced raining last evening shortly after dark and rained all night, waked up in the morning laying in a puddle of water, our pine shanty turning water in better than out; it was indeed a most disagreeable night."[17]

The inclement weather did not delay the continuation of the march on the morning of the 21st. It was still raining when the men left their camp between six and seven o'clock. The regiment tried to march on the roads but they were in terrible shape. The horses and wagons were stuck everywhere and the artillery was lodged in the mud. The progress in the "knee deep mud" was so slow that by twelve o'clock the men were ordered to pitch their tents for the night. The regiment had only gone three miles. Private Borland wrote at the end of the march: "It was fatiguing today and nearly the whole regiment straggled, indeed it was an army of stragglers."[18]

The wagons and the artillery experienced the most difficulty throughout the day. The roads were liquid, in many places, which caused these heavy vehicles to sink. In some instances, the mud actually covered the hubs of the wheels.[19] The teamsters tried to use mules and horses to pull the wagons and cannons from this quagmire. In some cases, 12, or as many as 16 horses or mules, were used to extricate these wagons from the mud.[20] But in many situations, these poor animals were unsuccessful in their attempts to move wagons, "spending most of their time keeping their heads above the water and mud."[21] Lieutenant D. Porter Marshall of the 155th humorously wrote many years after the march: "This is to notify all future explorers of this country, that if at any time they plow or dig up any U.S. army wagons or any batteries of artillery, they can credit [it] to 'Burnside's stick in the mud.'"[22]

To compound the problem, rations had not reached the regiment, and on January 22, the men were ordered to corduroy the roads. The initial work began with the pioneers and 50 men but soon escalated into the entire regiment's involvement. The men worked hard all day and returned to their camp at dark, without finishing the task. To add insult to injury, the regiment had to tolerate some heckling from their adversary. When the regiment came close to the stream, the Confederates on the opposite shore "hoisted signs with the inscription, 'Burnside stuck in the mud.'"[23]

The 23rd of January proved somewhat better for the men as the rations had reached the regiment and the corduroy roads were completed. The next morning, the men marched back to their old camp. The trek began at 9 A.M. and took almost four hours to traverse the approximate six miles the regiment had traveled since it left camp on January 20.

Upon arriving at their camp, the men confronted another major setback. While the regiment had been away, the stragglers and shirkers from the army had destroyed their campsite. Private Borland refused to let the situation upset him: ". . . [W]as really glad to see the old camp, although our quarters were demolished by some of the shirkers who remained in camp. We fixed up as well as we could and slept soundly on our pole bunk."[24] Burnside's inglorious march had finally come to an end.

With the mud march complete came the realization that the 123rd had participated yet again in another useless advance. In their relatively short history, the regiment had endured three useless marches: a forced march to Sharpsburg, only to arrive on the field the day after the battle; a march to Fredericksburg, only to be used as cannon fodder in a fruitless attempt to take an impregnable position; and Burnside's infamous mud march, which produced no tangible results.

In the following months, the regiment's "hard life" became a little easier. The brigade's campsite was moved to a new location which afforded the men many enjoyable amenities. These amenities, coupled with some much-needed rest, helped soothe some of the prior months' frustrations. The morale in the regiment steadily improved. As a result, these three months in early 1863 were remembered by almost all as their most pleasant time in the army.

CHAPTER SIX
WINTER QUARTERS—CAMP HUMPHREYS

And I will make them a covenant of peace and will cause
the evil hearts to cease out of the land; and they will dwell
safely in the wilderness, and sleep in the woods.

Ezekiel 34:24–25
Text of sermon by Chaplain H. L. Chapman, September 7, 1862

Since the regiment's return to camp, the weather began to improve, although the roads were still impassable. The men made the best of what appeared to be a long winter hiatus from action. For some, it was a positive break from the army's prior disappointments. Private Borland noted that he "lived gay for the last few days having butter, dried apples, bean soup, rice, condensed milk & c., almost made us forget soldiering."[1]

On January 26, the relative calm of the encampment was disrupted by an order to construct a new bivouac for the winter months. The new camp was named Camp Humphreys after the division commander. It took approximately one week to build, but by all accounts, the time was well spent and the new camp received glowing accolades from the members of the brigade. For once, the encampment had been laid out in approved military form. The locale contained a parade campus, company streets, officers' quarters, and quartermasters' tents. Sanitary problems, which had plagued the brigade's prior campsites, were greatly improved. Steps were taken to ensure that proper standards for drainage and sanitation were strictly followed. Overall, the men agreed that the camp was the best-constructed site that they had seen. One member of the brigade affectionately remembered "[t]he memories of good health and comforts and pleasant days

Camp Humphreys

This idyllic environment was the camp for the division for the months of February, March, and April.

Under the Maltese Cross

in this camp during February and March and a large part of April, 1863" were not soon forgotten.[2]

Although not as enthusiastic as his comrades, Colonel Clark approvingly described the camp and its surroundings:

> Our present camp is a new one, named in honor of our Division General. The location is good—the water is good and the wood is convenient. But there are so many troops closely encamped that the thickest forest soon disappears. The farmers in this part of Virginia, (if there ever should be) will have some difficulty if defining boundary lines and still more in enclosing plantations.[3]

The members of the 155th remembered that this was a healthy period for the men. The members recalled that "[t]he bugle call, 'Come and get your quinine! Come and get your quinine!' for those suffering from temporary or imaginary ailments, . . . met with few responses in this camp, and formed a marked contrast to the experience of sickness, disabilities and excuses from duty in preceding camps of the Division."[4]

The time spent in Camp Humphreys was both enjoyable and therapeutic for the regiment. It was the longest time that the unit spent in any one place during its entire enlistment. The food was plentiful and morale was never better. Soft bread, once a luxury, was now served three to four times a week. Vegetables, which in prior times were in short supply, were served regularly. The result was unquestionably a much happier and healthier army.

The newspaper accounts back in Allegheny County, however, erroneously wrote of the ill health of the regiment, which drew the ire of its colonel. The *Pittsburgh Post and Gazette* printed on February 18 that "Col. Clarke's [*sic*] 123d regiment now numbers but 429 effective men out of 1,016 when it left the city last summer. The number in the hospitals is very large."[5] Colonel Clark clearly disagreed with the foregoing account. In a letter dated February 16, two days before the publication of the above article, the colonel noted: "At no time period since we left Sharpsburg has the general health of the regiment been as good as at present."[6]

In all probability the discrepancy over the health of the regiment can be attributed to the local newspapers. Although some health problems had existed within the regiment, the newspaper accounts often exaggerated the seriousness of the situation. Many who were reported ill were not sick but were detailed to work in other areas and some were on furloughs at home. The newspaper accounts made no breakdown of the reasons for the men being away from the regiment. This misstatement caused many of the families back in Pittsburgh and Allegheny to unnecessarily worry about the health of their loved ones.

Because the *Gazette's* article on February 18 created unnecessary fears about the overall health of the regiment, the March 7 edition offered a more detailed explanation. The article noted that the regiment now totaled 893, with 653 present in the regiment. Of the missing soldiers, 123 were sick in the hospital, 104 were detailed with other duties outside the regiment, and 13 were on furlough. The article concluded:

> From the above it will be seen that the regiment is still quite vigorous as regards numbers, notwithstanding the severe losses sustained in the Battle of Fredericksburg, and the large amount of sickness consequent upon the inclement weather of the past two months.[7]

Another reason for the regiment's improved morale was the appointment of Major General Joseph Hooker as the commander of the Army of the Potomac. This appointment was necessitated by the resignation of General Burnside. To the men in the regiment, the appointment of a new commander was meaningless. Hooker was the third commander of the Army of the Potomac during their short military career. Private Hemphill best summed up the feelings of the regiment:

> We are under "old fighting Joe Hooker" though and I suppose he will put us through as hard as he can . . . I suppose you will laugh at me for talking so but there are plenty of others that talk the same way. I cannot say that I have as much room to complain as those in the regiments that have

to carry a gun and knapsack, but still I must say that it is a hard life, any way you take it.[8]

For the men in the nine-month regiments, the appointment of a new commander indicated the possibility of a new offensive. Thus far, every new leader had initiated an attack shortly after his appointment. With only three months of their enlistment remaining, most wanted to serve out their time and go home to their families. As such, the men sought to fill up the many hours and days left in their enlistments.

Similar to any military unit, most of their time was spent on military tasks such as picket duty and military reviews. The free time available was used differently by each soldier. Some read or wrote letters to loved ones back home. Others used their time to think of ingenious ways to procure the evil of all armies: alcohol.

As was common during the winter months, many of the officers were permitted to take a short furlough to visit family and friends. Colonel Allabach took his leave sometime during February. As the senior colonel in the brigade, Colonel Clark became the acting commander of the unit. As acting brigade commander, one of his daily tasks was to sign all requisitions for supplies. Colonel Clark made it very clear that he would not sign any requisitions for alcohol, except for urgent medical purposes.

The officers of the brigade were clearly upset with the colonel's position. They presented many urgent pleas for the much-needed "commissary" for treatment of their cramps and other sundry conditions. But the colonel refused to sign any of the vouchers except for one.

Alexander Carson, a lieutenant in Company D of the 155th, visited the colonel and presented such a compelling story of his depressed condition that the colonel set aside his scruples and signed the lieutenant's requisition for *one canteen* full of the coveted alcohol. With great satisfaction, the junior officer took the signed form to his quarters where he altered the formal requisition by placing the number 4 after the 1 so that the amended requisition read 14 rather than 1. The amended requisition was thereafter taken to the commissary where it was duly honored. The members of the 155th remembered that "the cramps and kindred diseases affecting so many officers of the One Hundred and Fifty-fifth, after a few doses of this sovereign remedy, disappeared like magic."[9]

The months of February, March, and April were also times of suffering and death in the regiment. During this period, the regiment again lost a number of its members to sickness and disease. In February, five men died of disease and five were discharged on surgeons' certificates.[10] During March, four more members expired and seven were untimely discharged.[11] Fortunately for the regiment, only one died and one was discharged in April.[12]

The regimental command structure was not immune to the debilitating effects of these many months in the field. During the time in winter camp, the regimental hierarchy again underwent some significant changes. As previously noted, Captain Henry Maxwell of Company K resigned on December 31, 1862. Sometime in March, Private Hemphill noted that Captain John Boyd of Company F also resigned, but in actuality, Captain Boyd was granted a medical discharge on March 7, 1863.[13] As a result of this discharge, Captain Boyd's first lieutenant was promoted to captain.

In early March of 1863, the court-martial of Major Hugh Danver was heard by a military tribunal and resulted in another change in the regimental command. The sickly major was charged with misbehavior before the enemy and leaving the field without permission. Colonel Clark, the chief prosecution witness, testified that he had not given the major permission to leave the field during the battle. Others, including the regimental surgeon, attested that the accused was clearly ill and not fit for duty and was justified in leaving the battle due to his infirmities.

After much testimony, the tribunal found the major "not guilty" of misbehavior in front of the enemy but guilty of leaving the field without permission. However, the board found that there were mitigating circumstances to the major's departure and recommended a light sentence. Major Danver was granted a special discharge from the army on March 31, 1863. Captain Charles Wiley of Company A succeeded the major as the regiment's third in command. The newly appointed major's brother, Ephraim Wiley, took command of Company A for the remaining five weeks of field duty.

Colonel John B. Clark

The "Fighting Preacher," dressed for the field.

Lang Collection

As a result, by March 31, 1863, one half of the companies in the regiment were now led by new commanders due to death, sickness, resignation, and discharge. Companies A, F, G, I, and K were under new leaders. Two of the three highest ranking officers in the regiment had been replaced. In spite of all these changes to the leadership, one constant still remained: John Barr Clark.

During the time spent at Camp Humphreys, Clark's influence grew in the eyes of the rank and file. He offered the men not only military guidance but counsel regarding their personal lives. Private Borland noted Clark's advice on April 19, when the colonel preached: "A good home is better than precious ointment and the day of our death than the day of our birth."[14]

Colonel Clark's period of guidance and leadership was coming to a close, as the regiment had only four short weeks left in its nine-month term. While most hoped that this time could be served without another battle, Private Hemphill penned the sentiment of most in the regiment: "[I]t is my opinion that 'Old Joe' is going to give them another 'ball' before [we] go home."[15]

CHAPTER SEVEN
BATTLE OF CHANCELLORSVILLE

I waited patiently for the Lord; he inclined to me and heard my cry. He drew me up from the desolate pit, out of the miry bog, and set my feet upon a rock, making my steps secure.

Psalm 40:1–2
Text of sermon by Chaplain H. L. Chapman, January 11, 1863

Private Hemphill's words proved prophetic as the regiment prepared for its final march to Chancellorsville. The months of March and April were a time of great planning for the Union high command. A new offensive was planned for the beginning of spring, and the rumors around camp were plentiful. On April 14, the regiment was ordered "8 days rations in [their] haversacks . . . and 20 rounds of ammunition." The men were instructed to take only essential clothing and to box up all extra apparel for delivery to the quartermaster.[1]

The men viewed the issuance of ammunition and rations as a sign that they were not moving to a peaceful locale. On no other previous campaign had the men been ordered to carry more than three days' rations. This order clearly signified that the regiment was moving away from its base of supplies and into an area where wagons could not readily supply the troops. It also indicated the probability that the fighting would last a number of days.

The number of men who were preparing for this march had been depleted by nine months of active campaigning. General Humphreys reported that 3,684 officers and men were present at the beginning of this new offensive. He further broke this number down into 1,616 enlisted men and 95 commissioned officers in Tyler's Brigade; and 1,865 enlisted men and 108 officers in

Allabach's command.[2] "Once 7000 strong, [the division now] had been reduced through the casualties of war."[3] As a result, close to one-half of the men who once made up this illustrious division would not participate in the upcoming campaign.

None of the men gave any indication that they feared the impending campaign. The regiment was now a battle-tested unit and the men were aware of the realities of war. That is not to say that they were anxious for the fight. Most of the men would have gladly served out their term in the safety of Camp Humphreys, but the nine-month men would participate in one final battle before their discharge.

The commanding general had already formulated his plan of attack. A number of coordinated movements were necessary in order for the plan to be successful. The strategy initially called for the cavalry corps to move up the Rappahannock and cross at the upper fords. Once across, the corps was to split into two columns—one to attack at Gordonsville and Culpeper and the other to move toward the Fredericksburg railroad with the intent of cutting off Lee's lines of communication and supplies. After this was successfully accomplished, both columns were to meet and harass Lee's army as it retreated from Fredericksburg.

The cavalry left camp, as planned, on April 13. But the weather did not hold and it began raining the night of April 14 and continued through the 15th. Private Borland recalled that it was the "hardest rain" the men experienced since they were mustered into service.[4] The steady downpour quickly flooded the upper fords, which caused the cavalry to delay its crossing until the 28th of April. This unexpected holdup rendered the cavalry useless in the upcoming campaign.

Similar to his predecessor, General Hooker did not despair over this sudden change of plan. On April 26, Hooker issued his orders for the forward movement of the infantry. His plan assumed that after the cavalry had cut off the Confederate supply line, the rebel forces would have only two viable options. The Union commander speculated that either Lee would abandon his strong position at Fredericksburg and retreat to the Orange and

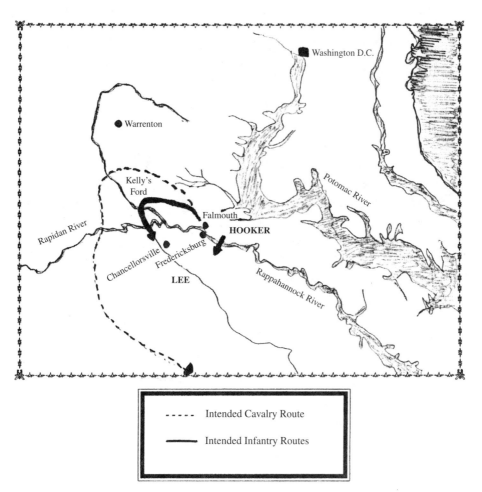

Hooker's Plan of Attack

Alexandria Railroad, or come out of his trenches and attack their superior numbers.

But before either of these options could play out, the Union had to cross its men over two rivers. On April 26, the pioneers from each division were sent to United States Ford to prepare for the crossings. On April 27, the regiment began its march. The trek started at 1 P.M. and proceeded for 8 to 9 miles until the men bivouacked for the night.[5] While the exact location of the campsite cannot be ascertained, it is known that the site was near Hartwood Church.[6] On April 28, the men were ordered to be in line at 7 o'clock, but the march did not begin until 9 A.M. The two-hour delay was caused by the passing of Franz Sigel's Division and the XII Corps. After these units had passed, the regiment took its proper place in line.[7] It rained considerably throughout the day and the roads were very muddy in some places. The regiment covered close to 15 miles before it finally stopped for the night.

On April 29, the regiment was on the move again. The First Division of the V Corps, Brigadier General Charles Griffith's Division, took the lead for the day. Major General George Meade, the new commander of the V Corps, directed General Humphreys and his division to bring up the trains and pontoons and supervise their crossing of the Rappahannock.[8] The 123rd did their job admirably, but was delayed in its crossing because of the massive amount of men and material congregated at the ford. The unit did not begin the unpleasant task of crossing the Rappahannock until after dark. It rained considerably during the night and the pontoons were wet and slippery.[9] As soon as the last man in the brigade had crossed, the pontoons were taken up and moved. It was close to 11:30 P.M. before all of the pontoons had been loaded and the train was ready to move to Ely's Ford. Due to the heavy rain, the marshy and sandy roads made traveling very difficult.[10] The division moved slowly and tried to catch up with the rest of the army.

After having completed the difficult night crossing, the men were confident that they would catch up with the army by morning. At 3 A.M., however, the guide who was leading the division realized that they were lost. Although this same guide had traveled this road on two other occasions throughout the day, he was unsure of the division's present location. The men tried to find their way to the ford, but the night was so dark that Humphreys was forced to call a halt until daylight.

The order to move came very early the next morning. The men started at daybreak and forded "Deep Creek." After reaching the opposite shore, the division continued the march until they reached the Rapidan River at Ely's Crossing in the early afternoon where they were ordered to wade across the river. The division initially responded with disbelief at this directive. The members of the 155th wrote: "At first the proposition that all the troops should wade the Rapidan at this ford seemed incredible, considering that the weather was quite cool and that the troops had become very warm by their fatiguing march."[11]

The crossing of the Rapidan was cold and difficult. Private Christian Rhein of the 123rd penned a description: "When we came to the river Rapidan, having nothing in which to cross it, we assumed the costume of Adam before he left Paradise, made a bundle of our clothes and put them with our guns on our heads and plunged boldly in. We got across all right, but the water was terrible cold and rapid."[12]

Upon reaching the southern banks of the Rapidan, the men marched another two miles and encamped for the night in a dense pine forest. The regiment had marched 18 miles and was 3 miles from Chancellorsville.[13] They settled in for a quiet rest, even though their clothes were wet and it rained all night.[14]

At dawn on May 1, the regiment continued its trek to Chancellorsville. The march was delayed by Tyler's brigade which was one hour late reporting for duty. General Humphreys was not pleased by the delay, yet even with this minor disruption, the men reached Chancellorsville by 7 A.M.[15] Upon arriving at the crossroads, the regiment was halted and their arms and ammunition inspected.[16] The inspection took place in an open field in the vicinity of the Chancellor House. At the time of the inspection Adjutant William P. McNary read Hooker's infamous order

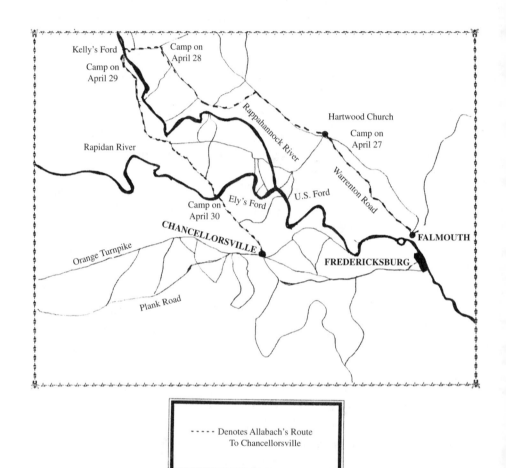

Kelly's Ford

Camp on
April 28

Camp on
April 29

Rappahannock River

Hartwood Church

Camp on
April 27

Rapidan River

Warrenton Road

Ely's Ford

U.S. Ford

Camp on
April 30

CHANCELLORSVILLE

FALMOUTH

Orange Turnpike

FREDERICKSBURG

Plank Road

----- Denotes Allabach's Route
To Chancellorsville

The 123rd's March to Chancellorsville

regarding the march to the regiment. He loudly proclaimed: "It is with heartfelt satisfaction that the last three days have determined that our enemy must ingloriously fly, or come out from behind their defenses and give us battle on our own ground, where certain destruction awaits him." The order had an uplifting effect on the men and "infused new life into [the] . . . weary bodies" of the soldiers.[17]

At approximately 11:30 A.M., Sykes' Division led a reconnaissance in the direction of Banks' Ford. Griffin's Division moved on the left down the River Road. Humphreys' men followed Griffin's Division and acted as a reserve for the movement. General Meade explained the deployment:

[On May 1], under orders of the major-general commanding, the corps was put en route to take position to uncover Banks' Ford, the left resting on the river, the right extending on the Plank Road. For this purpose, Sykes' division was ordered to advance on the . . . turnpike until after crossing

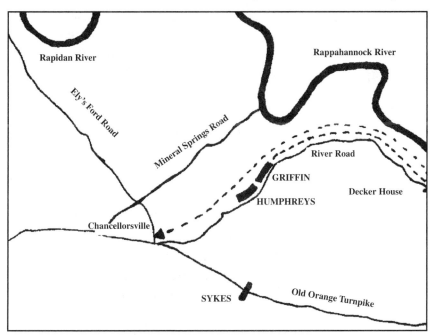

The 123rd's Line of March on May 1, 1863

Mott's Run, when he was to move to the left, deploy, and
open communication with Griffin on his left and Slocum on
his right, and, when all were in position to advance simulta-
neously against the enemy, supposed to be in position from
the Plank Road to the river. Griffin was ordered to move
down the River . . . Road until in the presence of the enemy,
when he was to deploy, his left resting on the river and his
right extending toward Sykes. Humphreys was ordered to
follow Griffin, to be held in reserve to re-enforce Griffin or
Sykes as the exigencies might require.[18]

After moving approximately a mile and one-half down the
road, Sykes' reconnaissance met the enemy's skirmishers. A spir-
ited engagement ensued during which Sykes drove his adversary a considerable distance down the road. These were the
opening shots of the battle.

Humphreys' and Griffin's Divisions were not sent to Sykes'
aid as was initially planned. Instead, after Sykes informed the
commanding general that he feared he was outflanked, he was
ordered to withdraw back to the safety of Chancellorsville. The
men of the division and army viewed this as the first sign that
"Fighting Joe Hooker" was losing his nerve.

Sykes' retrograde motion halted Hooker's offensive tactics
and relinquished the high ground, and Banks' Ford, to his adversary. With this retreat, Hooker surrendered the tactical initiative
and fought the remainder of the battle from a defensive position.
After the battle, many recognized this as Hooker's single most
costly error. If Hooker had taken and held Banks' Ford, he would
have shortened his lines of communication and supply by many
miles, which would have greatly helped in providing for the army
in the days ahead. Further, the move also yielded much of the
high ground that the army had already captured. As General
Meade later observed, ". . . if we can't hold the top of a hill, we
certainly can't hold the bottom of it."[19] The only answer General
Hooker could give for this move was that "for once I lost confidence in Hooker, and that is all there is to it."[20]

After nearly reaching the ford, Griffin's and Humphreys' divisions received the order to return to Chancellorsville. Upon arriving back at the Chancellor House, the men took a short rest from their exhausting march. The battle began to rage around the house as "men poured grape" into the advancing Confederates.[21] The battle was escalating when General Meade received orders to send Humphreys' Division back down the road to "occupy the extreme left of the line, on the river bank, and . . . hold the approach to the United States Ford by the . . . River Road, in force."[22] Although exhausted from their previous march, the men quickly answered the call. The four-mile-march was made in 40 minutes and was essentially a race between Humphreys' Division and the rebels.[23] Humphreys' Division won the march and held the position.

At dawn on May 2, there was "considerable shelling along the lines" and the brigade was ordered to construct "a line of breast works" and to "hold the position at all hazards."[24] The men worked diligently and in short order created a strong, defensible position. Along with the men from Humphreys' divisions, 26 pieces of artillery were placed on the hill.[25] This deployment effectively commanded the entire area in front of the line. The men were confident that they would be successful in case of an attack.[26]

The regiment watched as a body of the enemy began to gather in the woods, in plain sight of their position.[27] The woods were quickly shelled by the massed batteries, and the enemy was forced to retreat in haste.[28] As the men watched, they became increasingly anxious for the enemy to attack, since they now held the high ground and the entrenched position.[29]

But Lee did not aim his main attack at this part of the line. Early on May 2, the Confederate commander had ascertained that the Union right flank could be successfully attacked if he could move enough men across the Union front and strike the unsuspecting corps. Even though Lee realized that this move was against all conventional military wisdom, he opted to split his army. The only person Lee trusted for this monumental task

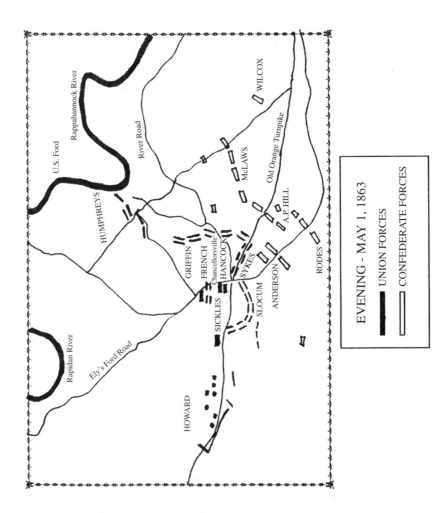

EVENING - MAY 1, 1863

UNION FORCES

CONFEDERATE FORCES

Troop Positions

Rappahannock River

U.S. Ford

River Road

Rapidan River

Ely's Ford Road

HUMPHREYS

WILCOX

McLAWS

Old Orange Turnpike

A.P. HILL

GRIFFIN

FRENCH

Chancellorsville

HANCOCK

SYKES

ANDERSON

RODES

SICKLES

SLOCUM

HOWARD

was his Second Corps Commander, General Thomas "Stonewall" Jackson.

General Jackson and his corps began the march at approximately 7:00 A.M. on the second. Throughout the day, Lee made scattered demonstrations all along the Union line, in hopes of masking his true intentions. While some reports trickled in during the day that a mass movement of Confederate troops was occurring, General Hooker opted to believe that General Lee had chosen to withdraw to Gordonsville and made no serious adjustments to his deployment.

Humphreys' Division saw little activity during the day, but the apparent calm was finally shattered at approximately 5:15 P.M. when General Jackson struck the right flank. Even though Humphreys' men were holding the opposite flank, they heard the fallout from this disastrous attack. General Robert E. Rodes, a division commander in the Confederate Second Corps, later wrote: "So complete was the success of the whole maneuver, and such was the surprise of the enemy, that scarcely any organized resistance was met with after the first volley was fired. They fled in the wildest confusion, leaving the field strewn with arms, accouterments, clothing and caissons, and field pieces in every direction."[30]

Upon hearing of the attack on the right, Assistant Surgeon William Shaw Stewart, along with his brother Samuel, immediately rode to the scene of the action. Surgeon Stewart attempted to stop these frightened soldiers:

> We turned our horses across the road, drew our swords and commanded a halt. At first the frightened crowd were so defiant that one man raised his gun and pointed it at my brother's breast, but he dropped it suddenly without firing . . . We succeeded in forming a line and were about getting the men turned back when suddenly a large drove of steers came dashing down the road at full speed, their drivers yelling at the top of their voices. This was enough to scatter the panic stricken soldiers into the woods, beyond our reach of control.[31]

While the men of the 123rd could not see the developing problem, they could clearly hear the "heavy firing on the right of [the] lines."[32] The right was collapsing and the men of the XI Corps were running in retreat. Because the attack occurred so late in the day, night soon covered the field and slowed the Confederate progress. As darkness came, the men could hear "scattered shots followed by the roar and crash of thousands of muskets."[33] Along with these sounds came the muffled shouts and cheers of the opposing army as they moved closer to the Union left. It was during one of these late evening flurries that General Stonewall Jackson was mortally wounded by his own troops and ultimately died of his wounds on May 10.

The men of the 123rd were not aware that General Jackson was wounded, but they were cognizant of the battle that filled the night of the second and the third. During the early morning hours of May 3, the division was ordered to begin its march to the right. The men quickly swallowed their coffee and hardtack and got in line for the march.

The men of the V Corps quickly marched to the battlefield over the very roads that they had traversed earlier. Upon their arrival on the field, they "[f]ormed in line of battle, by battalion"along the "Ely's Ford road [i]n the woods intervening between Chandler's and Chancellor's houses, [on] the ground previously occupied by a part of French's Division." General Meade placed "Griffin's division [on] the left of this line and Sykes the right, [with] Humphreys in reserve, massed in the rear of Sykes."[34]

At approximately 8 A.M., Allabach's brigade moved forward and formed "in line of battle, in the open field to the left of the white house [Chandler House]."[35] This new deployment placed the 123rd on the right flank of Humphreys' Division with its extreme right near the Chandler House. Shortly after this deployment was completed, a significant event occurred that was crucial to the future tactical decisions made by General Hooker.

Between 9 and 10 A.M., General Hooker was standing on the portico of the Chancellor House observing the developing battle.

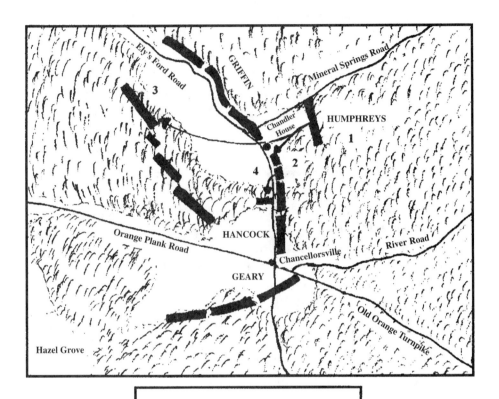

1. Humphreys' Position — 6:00 A.M.

2. Allabach's Brigade Position — 8:00 A.M.

3. Tyler's Brigade Position — 9:00 A.M.

4. Movement of the 131st and 155th —
   11:00 A.M.

Troop Positions May 3, 1863

Suddenly, a solid shot struck the pillar next to him, splitting it in two and causing one-half to strike the general on his right side. General Hooker noted that "for a few moments I was senseless . . . [b]ut I soon revived and . . . insisted on being lifted on my horse, and rode back toward the white house [Chandler] which subsequently became the center of my new position. Just before reaching it, the pain from my hurt became so intense that I was likely to fall, when I was assisted to dismount, and was laid upon a blanket spread out on the ground, and was given brandy."[36]

Although General Hooker had been hit, he did not relinquish command of the army. This error in judgment plagued him for many years to come. Hooker's somewhat erratic behavior led many to believe that he had been drunk on the day of the battle. This supposition was not difficult to believe as Hooker had a reputation for heavy drinking.

As a result of Hooker's erratic behavior, the *Harrisburg Patriot and Tribune* published a defamatory article on May 12, 1863, which the 123rd responded to in Hooker's defense. The article stated: "We have . . . reliable intelligence that Hooker was beastly drunk and totally incapacitated for command or anything else, on Sunday . . ."[37]

Upon hearing of this statement, the regiment convened a meeting where the following resolution was adopted:

> WHEREAS, . . . we, the members of the 123d Pennsylvania Volunteers, having been in a position to behold the conduct of our commander on that day . . . and therefore competent witnesses in the matter and whose united testimony will certainly be favorably received for its veracity, and whereas, we desire to express the truth for the information of the true men, as well as traitors, we do adopt the following resolutions, hoping that they may have their desired effect of setting forth the matter in its true light.
>
> . . . That the assertion of the Patriot and Union is an unqualified falsehood and a reproach thrown at the fair fame of our beloved General, acquired on a hard fought field, and not to be passed over in silence by those who have the power to

contradict such treasonable emanations from the contaminated fountain of treason.

. . . That as soldiers and country loving citizens, who have fought under Gen. Hooker . . . we are led to express our unbounded confidence in the generalship of our gallant commander to the country and to resent all attempts to tarnish the character of our leaders and thereby injure the interests of our country.[38]

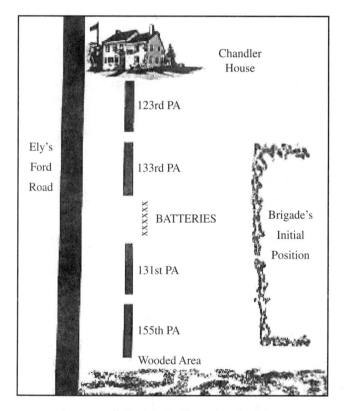

Allabach's Position May 3

Colonel Clark also denounced those who disparaged the reputation of General Hooker. In his farewell speech to the regiment, the colonel proclaimed:

When we came within the lines of the Potomac army, the first thing almost that met us was the broad declaration that the Commander of that army during the engagement of Sabbath, was beastly intoxicated. There is not a word of truth in it . . . The right of my regiment rested during the entire engagement within three rods of the Headquarters of General Hooker, and not fifteen minutes intervened during the entire engagement in which I did not see him. He was sober, serious and intent upon the work in hand. Whatever may be the impression among my fellow citizens in regard to him, I have this to say that, in him the Government has found an earnest, confiding man—one determined upon the destruction of the rebellion . . .[39]

But the eloquent defense of General Hooker by the entire 123rd, as well as Colonel Clark, fell on deaf ears. Many of Hooker's critics had already determined that he had been drunk. To them, this was the only logical reason for Hooker's sudden timidity in battle. And because of their acceptance of what appeared to be an obvious answer, many could not possibly accept any other explanations to the contrary.

After the division had been formed near the Chandler House, General Humphreys received orders to send a brigade to support General William H. French's division of the Second Corps on the right flank of the Union battle line. General Tyler's brigade was selected for this duty. But before Tyler's brigade moved to the front, General Humphreys addressed the division by stating: "You have come out to fight . . . you must fight and if you won't fight I'll make you fight."[40]

After Humphreys' address, Tyler's brigade moved to the northwest and formed on the extreme right of the Union battle line. The enemy opened fire on the group and General Tyler's brigade valiantly made a stand against the Confederate onslaught. The men held their ground for nearly an hour while they hoped for reinforcements. Tyler's men noticed that a large force in a "double line was plainly seen advancing and extending further to the right."[41] Faced with what appeared to be insurmountable odds and being outflanked on their right, the brigade slowly withdrew to its former position.

Meanwhile, Allabach's brigade was still occupying the open field to the left of the Chandler House. Stray shots and shells were dropping everywhere around the position and coming uncomfortably close to the brigade.[42] The "balls, shells, grape, [and] canister" were rattling through the woods, causing branches and limbs to fall all around the men.[43] The men lay low and hoped that the shelling would soon cease.

When the men did look up, the view from their position was spectacular. The Union line was beginning to collapse as the enemy was clearly winning the battle in and around Chancellorsville. General Hooker knew that a new, shorter line needed to be established around the Chandler House. In preparation for the withdrawal, General Meade began deploying close to "forty or fifty pieces of Union artillery"[44] under the command of Captain Stephen H. Weed.

At approximately 11 A.M., General Humphreys was ordered to place two of his regiments at the disposal of Major General Couch. The 133rd and the 155th were selected for this hazardous duty. Once the units were received by General Couch, they were placed perpendicular to the road leading to Chancellorsville, one on each side, and directed to advance to the edge of the woods bordering the open ground at Chancellorsville. This ground was now controlled by the enemy. General Humphreys explained that the object of the maneuver was to "hold the enemy in check until the two corps of Major General Couch and Daniel Sickles were placed in the new positions they were to occupy." Once these positions were taken, the two regiments were told to retire slowly through the woods and rejoin the brigade.[45]

At about 11 A.M., Colonel Allabach led the two regiments forward into the woods. They did not go far when they stopped and set up a defensive line. At this position, the detachment was quickly "under a severe fire of shell, grape, and canister."[46] Fortunately, the range of the Confederate "artillery and musketry was all above the heads of the prostrate men." The enemy soon ceased their firing and began to leave their breastworks and move forward toward Allabach's line. General Humphreys immediately saw the precarious nature of the position and ordered his men to promptly and rapidly retreat "so that the fifty-four pieces of artillery under Captain Stephen H. Weed could let loose their fire on the pressing foe." The movement was perfectly executed and the pursuing Confederates were greeted with a destructive volley which left many dead and wounded in the woods to the front.[47]

The two detached regiments, along with the rest of the brigade, moved in mass back to the "ground of the first formation" and formed "by battalion[s]." After remaining in this position for only a short time, the brigade shifted "to the right and rear of the Regulars, as . . . support" for this division.[48] Private Ross recorded that at "[a]bout five o'clock [we] filed into the woods."[49]

This concluded the brigade's fighting for the day. All that remained for the men, on the evening of the third, was to endure the suffering of their fellow soldiers. Christian Rhein vividly recalled the scene along the march:

> I was a Corporal at that time, and sent a squad into the woods in our front to do some skirmishing. We advanced very cautiously from tree to tree. The woods were full of Union and Confederate wounded and after going some distance I heard someone cry out, "For God's sake, help me." I looked around and found a young man belonging to some Ohio regiment who said he offered to surrender when the reb ran a bayonet into him. I called a couple of my comrades and we took him to the edge of the woods, where we left him, as we were obliged to return into the woods again . . . The woods were soon on fire, whether accidentally or otherwise . . . The cries that went up from the poor wounded were heart-renching [sic].[50]

But for the members of the regiment, the day's fight was finished. And in truth, the 123rd's term of enlistment was also completed the following day. But the members of the regiment elected to stay with the division until the battle was concluded. General Humphreys, in his after-battle report, specifically singled out the men of the 123rd for their resolve to see the battle through.

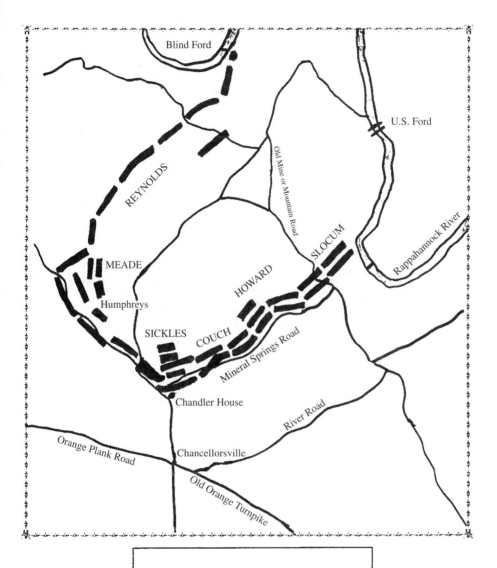

**Position Evening of May 3 and
Morning of May 4, 1863**

Troop Positions

As for the casualty count on the third, the regiment was extremely lucky having no deaths and a small number of wounded. While the men had not been actively engaged during the day, they were almost continually, during the late morning and early afternoon, exposed to artillery shelling. Private Ross penned that "[s]ome 3 or 4 in our regiment [were] wounded."[51] Bates wrote in his history that "seven men were wounded by the explosion of a single shell."[52]

Although the battle had ended, the regiment's military duties were not yet over. The men of the 123rd would spend another two days on the southern side of the Rappahannock before their retreat to Falmouth. The men saw no further fighting but had to endure some further sleepless nights before their discharge from the army.

On May 4, the division received a number of conflicting directives. Before daylight, General Humphreys received orders to support General Daniel Sickles, on the left, if certain events transpired. In obedience to these orders, the general detached a group of men to open up a route through the thick underbrush to this position. Later in the day, the general received further orders to support General Reynolds, on the right, and also opened up a route to this position.[53] But fortunately for the men of the 123rd, the regiment was not called to support either of these positions. As Private Ross wrote in his diary: "Battle not renewed yet by either sides but there is considerable picket firing on the right. Was out to day repairing roads . . . There has been 3 days incessant hard fighting at this place. I believe it is called Chancellorsville Cross Roads . . . The rebs must either come out and fight us on our own ground or retreat."[54]

The rebel army, however, did not do what Private Ross had anticipated. The Confederates had clearly won a great victory on the first two days of the battle, and Lee was not about to jeopardize this triumph with a precipitative offensive maneuver. The Confederate leader did send some of his troops to attack the VI Corps which was in an isolated position to the west of Fredericksburg. This action took place in the vicinity of Salem Church on the Plank Road outside Fredericksburg.

By way of background, Major General John Sedgwick and his VI Corps had attacked Marye's Heights on May 3 and had been successful in carrying the heights. On May 4, after having spent the evening of the third in the vicinity of Salem Church, Sedgwick became aware that a significant Confederate force was amassing on three of his fronts. He urgently requested General Hooker for reinforcements, but the commanding general was of the opinion that he had no men to spare. As such, Sedgwick did the best he could, but retreated across the Rappahannock that evening, relinquishing the heights which Humphreys' Division had so valiantly attempted to carry in December. While Private Ross wrote in his diary, "[i]t is rumored that Sedgwick with the 6th corps has taken Fredericksburg and the heights surrounding,"[55] the report was only half true. By the evening of the fourth, Fredericksburg was back in the hands of the Confederates.

On the morning of the fifth, the 123rd, along with the remainder of the division, moved to the right and formed as a reserve to Sykes' line. In the afternoon, by direction of Major General Meade, Allabach's brigade was formed in line of battle 150 yards in rear of Sykes' left, and Tyler's brigade 100 yards in rear of Allabach's. The corps commander instructed the general that if the enemy entered the intrenched line, the division was to charge with the bayonet. This position was occupied by the division until it was ordered to march to United States Ford.[56]

The afternoon and evening of the fifth were unpleasant for the men. It rained hard for most of the afternoon and the men were forced to lay in the mud, in line of battle, very close to the Confederate lines.[57] Due to the close proximity, the men could not start a fire and were forced to endure the wet and cold of the night.[58] Private Ross summed up the evening by saying: "It was a dark wet night."[59]

But the weather did not hamper the operations of the army. At nightfall, the army began its retreat to the northern side of the Rappahannock. The V Corps, as in the prior campaign, formed the rear guard for the retreating forces. At nightfall, General Humphreys detailed two of the regiments from the division to "aid [in] the passage of the artillery as far as the United States Ford."[60] The 123rd was one of these regiments. The men left their camp at 10 o'clock and were "up all night."[61]

The division, as a whole, commenced its march to the ford at approximately one in the morning. In the distance, the men could see the glow of the commissary stores that had been burnt by their own forces. After proceeding only one mile, the division was halted and massed on the right of the road leading to the ford. The men remained at this location until daylight when they were moved to a new position with their left resting on River Road and their right on the outbuildings around United States Ford. Once Griffin's division took up a position in the division's rear, the men were ordered to cross the Rappahannock on the upper pontoon bridge while Sykes' division crossed on the lower.[62]

The men marched another 12 miles after the crossing before they reached their old camp. The division, in toto, arrived in camp by dusk on the sixth. The Chancellorsville Campaign was now over. For the men of the 123rd, there was a silver lining to the entire affair. Their term of enlistment was now complete and they were going home. The men must have felt a certain amount of pride in what they had accomplished during their nine months in the field. But tantamount in their minds, at this point, was getting home. While they spent another two days in camp before their departure, their military duties, for all practical purposes, were completed.

For the regiment, the Chancellorsville Campaign had produced a minimal amount of casualties. Clearly their casualties in this battle—two men wounded and six men listed as missing— were significantly less than their losses in their first encounter with the enemy.

The regiment could clearly take solace in the fact that it had again "seen the elephant." General Humphreys paid the men the highest compliment when he wrote in his after-battle report: "I cannot close this report without expressing my gratification at the fine spirit that animated my division throughout the recent operations. Long marches, rapid movements, long-continued labor in opening roads and throwing up entrenchments, exposure to heavy and continuous rain, loss of rest, all combined, did not destroy their cheerfulness nor dampen their spirits. They exhibited the same courage in meeting the enemy that they formerly shown, and under circumstances that are recognized as unfavorable to the exhibition of the best quality of troops."[63] The men had finally made their commander proud.

Chapter Eight
Coming Home

It is finished.

The two remaining days in the field were filled with the necessary preparations for the regiment's departure for home. In fact, of the eight regiments that comprised Humphreys' Division since its inception in September, all but the 91st and 155th Pennsylvania were leaving the army. These two regiments were transferred to another division during the middle of May.

The men of the 123rd were anxious to return to their homes. On May 7, they shared one last moment with the remainder of the brigade. Some of the departing members decided to play a practical joke on their commander. They gathered all of the cartridges they could find, and with some of the powder, laid a mine near General Humphreys' tent. They ignited the powder and made a quick getaway to watch the ensuing melee. The detonation was loud and scattered cans and bottles in the vicinity of General Humphreys' tent. The general, not known for his sense of humor, was extremely upset when he found out that the entire incident was a rouse. He called out the provost guard and created quite a commotion in camp. One member later noted: "It was generally supposed that if the General had possessed power . . . he would have enjoyed . . . the duty of shooting a couple of battalions of the nine months regiments . . ."[1]

Although General Humphreys may have been upset at the division's most recent antics, in reality, the division commander had grown extremely fond of his men. In his last report as the commander of the division, he proudly declared:

In making this my last report of the operations of my division as at present constituted, I trust I may be excused for

138

recurring to the services it has performed. Hastily organized in September last near Washington, the regiments newly raised, it made a long and painful march of more than 23 miles in a dark night to take part in the expected battle of the next day at Antietam. When in camp the officers and men have been zealous in their efforts to acquire a knowledge of the duties of the soldier. They have cheerfully performed every duty required of them, whether that of the working party or armed service. They have been prompt and obedient, and have fought as well as the best troops at Fredericksburg and Chancellorsville. The task of instruction has been a heavy one to me, but I have the satisfaction of knowing that my efforts have not been without good results.[2]

The men appreciated General Humphreys' sentiments as they prepared for their departure home. On May 8, the 123rd was drawn up in line, with the rest of Allabach's brigade, and tendered a fond farewell. While no record exists depicting the exact nature of this gathering, a member of the brigade noted that many "[c]heers were given and farewells . . . spoken."[3]

While the members of the 155th were clearly happy for their fellow comrades from Pittsburgh, the march to the train station exacerbated an already rampant case of homesickness. The men of the unit undoubtedly asked the members of the 123rd to pass along their fond wishes to their family and friends back in Allegheny County. For some of these families, this would be the last communication they would receive from their loved one from the field.

The regiment left the depot at Stoneman's Switch on May 8 and began what would become an eight-day journey home. The regiment arrived in Harrisburg some time on May 9 and expected to be back in Allegheny County by May 10. But the slow and tedious mustering out process took much longer than had originally been anticipated. By May 12, only Companies E, H, and G had been mustered out.[4]

These last few days of waiting brought about the last casualty to befall the members of the 123rd. On May 14, the *Pittsburgh*

Colonel Clark Leads the Regiment Home

Under the Maltese Cross

Gazette gave the first inkling of the tragedy: "We regret to learn that Andrew McKain, a member of the 123d Regiment, Col. Clark, was accidentally killed in Harrisburg, this morning, just previous to the departure of the three o'clock A.M. train for the city. He was on the track as the train approached this depot, and was run over and instantly killed. We have no other particulars."[5]

Private McKain had been a musician with Company B and lived in the Second Ward of Allegheny City. He was a butcher by trade and left a wife and family to be cared for after his death. On May 16, the circumstances of Private McKain's death were sadly reported to the citizenry:

> On Wednesday morning, between two and three o'clock, just as the Baltimore Express train was leaving the depot, a soldier jumped upon the track and commenced beckoning to the engineer as if to stop the train. Before any notice could be taken of him by the engineer or the fireman, he was struck by the locomotive and literally cut to pieces, and instantly killed. His body was a mere mass of torn flesh and broken bones, so suddenly and severely was he struck by the cowcatcher and wheels of the locomotive. It was conjectured that

he desired to get upon the train, as there was nothing on the track which endangered the train, in order to attract the attention of the engineer.[6]

But the loss of Private McKain did not dampen the spirits of the families back home. Even though the residents of Pittsburgh and Allegheny City were unclear on when the regiment would arrive, they were enthusiastically planning a parade in their honor. The only problem was when it would take place. The suspense ended on May 14 when Colonel Clark telegraphed the city that the unit would be home on Saturday, May 16, on the 9:30 A.M. train. The loved ones and citizens of both cities could not be happier.

The long anticipated day finally arrived as the residents waited for the regiment's arrival. A detachment of the Pennsylvania Minute Men formed at the station to welcome the men. A number of fire companies waited in the streets to lead the preplanned parade. Both the mayor of Allegheny City and the mayor of Pittsburgh were with the large crowd that was anxiously awaiting the first glimpse of the train. After what seemed like hours, the engine finally came into view. In every window of the train, a soldier was hanging out waving to the crowd and scanning the massive throng for a familiar face. A reporter for the *Gazette* witnessed the event and wrote: "Such running, shoving, jamming, crushing, hunting, handshaking, hugging and kissing we never before witnessed. Every man, woman and child seemed to be in search of a soldier whom they could take to their embrace, and although all did not succeed, it was not for want of trying."[7]

The welcoming scene at the depot did not last long. Shortly after the train's arrival, the order to "fall in" was loudly given to the men. After the regiment had formed, the remaining members of the unit began their march to city hall. During the march and at the hall, a reporter for the *Pittsburgh Post* wrote of the many touching scenes he observed:

> When the procession formed, wives rushed into the ranks and marched side by side with their husbands. One lady had a little daughter, a child about eight or nine years of age.

When it saw its father, it sprang convulsively into his arms, and would not be separated from him, and this husband and wife, marched side by side, carrying their child. A handsome little boy, made his way into the hall, and singling out his brother, sprang towards him, and in a moment had his knap-sack, canteen, etc. stripped from his shoulders, and the next was heaping up in front of his plate everything he could lay his hands on.[8]

But not all the scenes during this day were joyous. For the households who had lost men in the field, the celebration was bittersweet. They undoubtedly were happy for the good fortunes of the families whose husbands, brothers, and sons had returned home. But they also could not help but feel a tremendous void for their own "empty chair." To these families, this joyous celebration was a harsh reminder of the unfairness of war.

But for most of the families, the return was indeed a delight-ful time. After the men had done "ample justice" to the provided meal, an order to "fall in" was given and the men proceeded to the West Commons of Allegheny where they were officially wel-comed back by the Honorable Thomas M. Howe.[9] Upon the regiment's arrival, Mr. Howe delivered a welcoming address. The former congressman captured many of the feelings of the as-sembled crowd:

Gentlemen of the 123d Pennsylvania Volunteers:

The grateful duty has been assigned to me of giving utter-ance to the joyful emotions which this day swell the bosoms of thousands of your fellow citizens, assembled to greet your return to your families and your homes. In their name, there-fore, I desire to bid you welcome, and with them to unite in acclamations of thanksgiving to the Great Ruler of events for the signal manifestation of his protecting care, with which everywhere marked your eventful military career.

The regiment has a history peculiar to itself. But ten short months ago the most of you were quietly occupied by your several professional and business pursuits . . . You had each one in his heart of hearts, quietly but firmly resolved, that whenever the exigency should arise requiring your services you would be ready to respond with alacrity which should impart an emphasis to the earnestness of your devotion. The reverses to our arms before Richmond . . . told you in language not to be mistaken, that the time had fully come—and lo! this regiment was born in a day.

You found your gallant Colonel at the sacred desk—unused to the "pomp and circumstance" of martial life . . . Ignoring the suggestions of a weak ambition, and inspired by the same patriotic impulse which animated you, he proposed to follow you to the tented field as your Chaplain and spiritual adviser, if it should be deemed improper to assign him the captaincy of his hundred men, for which his position he had first been indicated. My official relations enabled me to present his case in person to the Governor, who promptly intimated his purpose that he should be your Colonel—an intimation most happily in entire accord of the wishes of all of you. I have never been able, however, to divest my mind of the belief that he was assigned to that particular position by a Higher Power.

On this very spot, nine months ago, I witnessed the marshaling of this regiment for its departure to the seat of war, and saw your serried ranks, as one by one they moved with martial tread, amid the wild huzzas and acclamations of the multitude. I stood in thoughtful silence, scarce able to repress a tear, as I contemplated the sad necessity which called you forth, and felt that some were destined never to return . . . Fredericksburg and Chancellorsville will henceforth distinguish your Regimental Flag, and commend the noble corps which bore it on those bloody fields to the gratitude of posterity . . . And now let me ask you, in conclusion, if you have ever reflected how it has happened that amid all the perils through which you have passed, so few have fallen by casualties on the field of battle?

No similar number of men subjected to like exposure, have been so wonderfully preserved. It did not happen so—God has been your protector in answers to the prayers of the praying officers, and praying men, and praying friends at home—and to Him, the Triune God, alone should be ascribed unceasing thanks.[10]

At the conclusion of Mr. Howe's speech, the assembled crowd heartily applauded his oration.

But the next speaker was the individual the crowd most wanted to hear. Colonel John B. Clark, the minister-soldier, arose and addressed the assemblage. But for once in the colonel's long history of public oratory, he was unprepared to issue a lengthy speech. He explained to the crowd that the labors of the past few days had greatly fatigued him and he was not in the position to make a lengthy speech.[11] He did, however, defend the actions of General Hooker in the recent battle and gave a final farewell to his beloved regiment:

Gentlemen of the 123d Regiment, the relations sustained by me to you, and by you to me, are now dissolved. The nine months have gone into eternity; and here before these witnesses, it affords me pleasure to bear testimony of your good conduct and your strict conformity to all orders which were issued by me, or which came from higher authority. Now, gentlemen, soldiers, I bid you an affectionate farewell. Your highest, holiest and noblest aim will be to be good soldiers of Christ. My dear friends, farewell; and if forever fare thee well.[12]

The colonel then concluded his remarks in a manner appropriate to his civilian profession—by offering the blessings of the church—and the 123rd was no more.

In its relatively short history, the 123rd had faced many of the perils of a Civil War regiment. It had participated in two major battles and had endured the many hardships of the field and the march. Sixty men had been lost to disease and battle and 125 men had been wounded or missing.

Horatio K. Tyler

Horatio K. Tyler in his later years. He was very active in local politics and was appointed the government pension agent for the North Side of Pittsburgh.

Pittsburgh Post

Although Captain Tyler would serve in five regiments during the war, he would only list on his simple soldier's gravestone his involvement with the 123rd.

Photograph by Author

For some men, their mustering out from the 123rd was the end of their military careers; for others, it was only the beginning. Captain Horatio K. Tyler quickly enlisted in another regiment and ultimately served with two other units before his discharge in 1865.[13] Lieutenant Reuben Bartley of Company G joined the Signal Corps and became an integral part of Dahlgren's Raid on Richmond.[14] Sergeant Samuel Taggart was appointed a captain in the 116th Pennsylvania and lost his life at Ream's Station in 1864.[15]

In the coming years some from the division and regimental hierarchy entered the military, while others focused on their civilian lives. General Humphreys went on to further glory in the field and ended the Civil War as a corps commander. He resumed his career as the commander of the topographical engineers until his death in December of 1883 at the age of 73. Colonel Allabach returned to his home in Luzerne Township and resumed his dental practice. In 1873, he was appointed a captain in the United States Capital Police; a position he held until his death in 1893. Colonel Clark recruited another regiment, the 193rd Pennsylvania, in 1864 and spent another one hundred days in the field. Upon his discharge, he resumed his ministerial duties, eventually rising to a number of key positions in the Presbyterian Church. On January 13, 1872, the colonel died suddenly at his home in Allegheny at the age of 44. For Lieutenant Colonel Richard Dale, the second in command of the regiment, his life was far shorter than his commander's. In April of 1864, Lieutenant Colonel Dale was appointed as the lieutenant colonel of the 116th Pennsylvania. On May 12, 1864, due to the incapacity of the colonel of the regiment, Colonel Dale led the regiment's early morning charge at Spotsylvania and lost his life.

For most of the men, the years following the war brought prosperity and a slow-fading memory of their time in the army. The tales from the battles of Fredericksburg and Chancellorsville began to take a backseat to the more successful campaigns of the war. But the efforts of the men in Humphreys' Division were not totally forgotten. On November 8, 1908, the men of the division were called together one last time to commemorate their exploits at the dedication of their monument. The monument honoring Humphreys' Third Division was to be dedicated at the Fredericksburg National Cemetery.

An act of the Pennsylvania General Assembly assured that there would be a large turnout. The act authorized the payment of transportation fees for all honorably discharged veterans from the division. Captain Horatio K. Tyler, William Witherow, Frank P. Kohen, Bascom B. Smith, Andrew S. Miller, Captain John S. Bell, and many others from the 123rd attended the event.[16]

Colonel Clark's Grave

The colonel's body was sent back to his hometown of Cadiz, Ohio, where he was laid to rest by his mother. The monument was erected by his church and members of the 123rd and simply reads: "Our Pastor and Colonel."

Photograph by Author

The day began with a parade through the streets of Fredericksburg. The old soldiers, most in their late sixties and early seventies, marched proudly through the streets where they once sought cover, while thousands of local residents watched the mile-long parade. Governor Edwin S. Stuart of Pennsylvania led the cavalcade to the cemetery for the formal unveiling of the statue and told the gathered crowd of local residents: "You have Fredericksburg, and we have Gettysburg, where the men of Virginia and the men of Pennsylvania met in a later time, in opposing armies—each evidencing the highest qualities of the American soldier."[17] Colonel Alexander McClure, the primary speaker of the day, eloquently remembered the charge: "Hopeless as it seemed to the soldiers who made the assault with the officers in advance of the men, either to gain the heights or to hold them if gained, these Pennsylvania brigades started with hearty cheers to face the grim reaper of death: Next to Pickett's Charge at Gettysburg, [this charge] was the most bloody and disastrous assault of our Civil War." He cautioned the crowd that "we are not here to discuss the wisdom of army commanders" but to praise the men of "Pickett's Charge at Gettysburg and Humphreys' Charge at Fredericksburg" since "both stand in history, and will ever so stand, as high-water marks of heroism of American soldiery."[18] The attending veterans heartily applauded the comments of the colonel as they reflected on their days of youth.

The men of the 123rd in attendance, for one small moment, were not forgotten but remembered for their achievements. Many walked around the cemetery to say one final good-bye to their fallen comrades. Some deposited sprigs of evergreen on the forgotten graves of their friends. As the ceremony concluded, the entire gathering sang "Auld Lang Syne."[19] Many limped away, with cane in hand, to return to their homes in Allegheny and Pittsburgh. For most, this was the last time they saw these hallowed grounds. For all, it was the last time they answered the roll call as the men of the 123rd Pennsylvania.

Humphreys' Monument

The monument was dedicated on November 8, 1908.
Many of the members of the 123rd accepted the state's
invitation to attend and were present at the dedication.

Under the Maltese Cross

Every attendee from the division received a medal
commemorating Humphreys' Pennsylvania
Division.

Photograph by Author

APPENDIX A
CASUALTIES BY COMPANY FOR THE 123RD

STONE WALL

SCATTERED TROOPS FROM
PRIOR ASSAULTS

PROTECTIVE HILL

Left Wing

Company B	Company G	Company K	Company E	Company H
MURPHY	BOISOL	MAXWELL	BELL	DRUM
Killed	Killed	Killed	Killed	Killed
Alexander Dimler	None	None	Alexander Dallas	Cyrus Gold
William Dillon				
John Herman				
Wounded	Wounded	Wounded	Wounded	Wounded
Charles Palmer	Capt. Boisol	David Morrison	Mertin Rupert	B. Guthrie
Adelphus Lappe	William Harper	James Charlton	Hezekiah Johnston	Thomas Cargo
Lewis Rieb	J. M. Norris	Isaac Lapham	James Ramsay	John Seville
Lewis Young	Andrew McKnight		William Kelday	John Kirk
Andrew Robinson	William Ralston			Edward Kirk
Davis Owens	George Frazier			John Petts
				John Gillem
				Joseph Linton
				James Bambersoa
				James Milliken
				Sylvan. Samonton

Colors
(between Company H and Company C)

150

Right Wing

Company C ADAMS	Company I HUMES	Company D TYLER	Company F BOYD	Company A WILEY
Killed	Killed	Killed	Killed	Killed
John R. Munden	Lt. James Coulter	Nicholas Bandy	Sgt. Daniel Kipp	None
	Robert Reed	Joseph Heiserer	William Mehaffey	
	James McLaughlin	Henry Jenkins	George Walter	
	John McIntyre	August Mundel		
	W. S. Tantlinger	John Montague		
		George Wacenhuth		
Wounded	Wounded	Wounded	Wounded	Wounded
George Dilworth	Capt. Humes	Capt. H. K. Tyler	Capt. John Boyd	A. Cameron
David Beatty	Lt. S. D. Karns	Samuel Cestor	Sgt. James Boyd	John Chalfant
Alex. Altman	M. Ashbaugh	Michael Lanagan	Sgt. John Kennedy	Oscar J. Wright
Albert Boyce	J. Bailey	William Atherton	Corp. R. Walker	F. Miller
James Boyce	J. L. Black	John Ramsey	Corp D. Borland	John A. Graham
John Bradley	George Brush	John E. Shaller	John Agey	J. A. Whitehead
A. Hollander	John Casserly	Sam. McChesney	Joseph Alter	A. McCann
Christian Haber	Robert Gilley	James Russell	Mathew Byers	S. A. Barr
Henry Marsh	J. H. Lewis	Sgt. D. McGraw	Samuel Hunter	Joseph Helmup
Chas. McTiernan	James McCallup	Sgt. R. Graham	David Girt	E. J. Carpenter
S. Reynolds	Tom McConaha	Cor. Lingenfelter	William McKee	J. C. Hitch
George Stedeford	Daniel McMunn	Chas. Myers	D. B. Singer	
W. J. Smith	William Ross	A. C. Shaffer	W. Calpus	
Jacob Solar		Amos Coffer	Henry Arnold	
J. B. Stevens		Barney Shortman	James Ewing	
Wm. Worthington		John Ulman	John Wincher	
		Geo. Oulsma	George Walter	
		Henry Kaufman	William Shearer	
			Daniel F. Shaner	

APPENDIX B
HUMPHREYS' DIVISIONAL LOSSES, MARYE'S HEIGHTS

Command	Killed	Wounded	Missing	Total
1st Brigade				
91st PA	9	46	20	75
126th PA	12	66	14	92
129th PA	17	100	22	139
134th PA	14	109	25	148
2nd Brigade				
123rd PA	19	105	11	135
131st PA	22	138	15	175
133rd PA	20	145	19	184
155th PA	6	58	4	68
TOTALS	**119**	**767**	**130**	**1,016**

The totals here come from Humphreys' report in the *Official Records* with adjustments made for known errors. The casualty numbers are higher than those reported by Bates in his exhaustive study, but it is clear that Bates did not report all the losses. For example, if Bates is used for the 123rd, the casualty count would only be 65. This is clearly well below the numbers reported either in Humphreys' report or the *Gazette*. Since both of these accounts have relatively the same number of casualties and were written right after the battle, these are the more reliable figures.

Appendix C

Highest Divisional Losses,
Army of the Potomac at Fredericksburg

Division	Killed	Wounded	Missing	Total
Hancock	219	1,581	229	2,029
Meade	175	1,241	437	1,853
Gibbon	141	1,024	102	1,267
French	89	904	167	1,160
Humphreys	119	767	130	1,016
Sturgis	94	827	86	1,007

Casualties compiled from *Official Records*.

APPENDIX D
HIGHEST BRIGADE LOSSES,
ARMY OF THE POTOMAC AT FREDERICKSBURG

	Killed	Wounded	Missing	Total
Caldwell's Brig. Hancock's Div.	108	729	115	952
Jackson's Brig. Meade's Div.	56	410	215	681
Magilton's Brig. Meade's Div.	65	426	141	632
Ward's Brig. Birney's Div.	79	397	153	629
Allabach's Brig. Humphreys' Div.	67	446	49	562
Meagher's Brig. Hancock's Div.	50	421	74	545
Zook's Brig. Hancock's Div.	60	427	40	527
Kimball's Brig. French's Div.	36	420	64	520
Hall's Brig. Howard's Div.	63	419	33	515

Casualties compiled from *Official Records*.

APPENDIX E
CASUALTY FIGURES FOR MARYE'S HEIGHTS

Unit	Killed	Wounded	Missing	Total
II Corps				
1st Division				
Hancock	219	1,581	229	2,029
2nd Division				
Howard	104	718	92	914
3rd Division				
French	89	904	167	1,160
IX Corps				
2nd Division				
Sturgis	94	827	86	1,007
3rd Division				
Getty	16	216	64	296
V Corps				
1st Division				
Griffin	73	733	120	926
3rd Division				
Humphreys	119	767	130	1,016
TOTALS	**714**	**5,746**	**888**	**7,348**

The above numbers are taken from the *Official Records* with adjustments being made for known errors.

APPENDIX F
CASUALTY FIGURES FOR PICKETT'S CHARGE

Unit	Killed	Wounded	Missing	Total
Pickett's Division	500	2,007	375	2,882
Pettigrew's Division	470	1,893	337	2,700
Trimble's Division	155	650	80	885
TOTALS	**1,125**	**4,550**	**792**	**6,467**

The above numbers have been taken from George R. Stewart's analysis of the losses which were published in his book, *Pickett's Charge—A Microhistory of the Final Attack at Gettysburg, July 3, 1863*. While the casualty numbers noted for this attack have fluctuated over the years, the above figures appear to be the best guess as to the appropriate losses.

NOTES

INTRODUCTION

1. J. Watts De Peyster, "The Army of the Potomac—Gen. Humphreys at Fredericksburg," *The Historical Magazine* (June, 1869): 363.

2. *Dedication of Monument Erected By Pennsylvania To Commemorate The Charge of General Humphreys' Division, Fifth Corps, Army of the Potomac on Marye's Heights, Fredericksburg Virginia, December 13th, 1862—Dedicatory Ceremonies, November 11th, 1908* (Philadelphia: Press of J. B. Lippincott Company, 1908), 24.

3. "Letter from Col. Clark," *Pittsburgh Gazette*, October 24, 1862.

CHAPTER 1
Historical Background

1. On June 21, 1862, Governor Curtin issued a proclamation for 21 regiments of volunteers. He believed that the War Department had approved a number of these regiments as nine-month regiments. Unfortunately, in the end of June, he received word from the War Department that the initial permission had been revoked, "on the ground that the time of service was too short to be effective." This communiqué was again reversed on July 24, 1862, and the nine-month men were accepted into service. W. A. Love and W. H. Hartzell, *Organization of the Military of Allegheny County* (Pittsburgh: Privately Published, 1862), 36.

2. James M. McPherson, *Battle Cry of Freedom: The Civil War Era* (New York: Ballantine Books, 1989), 492.

3. "Letter from a Nine Months Beauty," *Pittsburgh Gazette,* March 17, 1863.

4. "The Great Mass Meeting," *Pittsburgh Gazette*, July 25, 1862.

5. "Filling Up," *Pittsburgh Dispatch*, July 30, 1862.

6. "Recruiting in the City," *Pittsburgh Dispatch*, August 1, 1862.

7. "Letter from Col. Clark," *Pittsburgh Gazette*, October 24, 1862.

8. "A Company of Presbyterians," *Pittsburgh Gazette*, August 8, 1862.

9. Ibid.

10. "Recruiting in the City," *Pittsburgh Dispatch*, August 8, 1862. Captain Gast's company mustered 103 men. Captain Adams' unit had enrolled 101 men. The company of Captain Tyler had 93 recruits.

11. James B. Ross diary, entry for August 10, 1862. James B. Ross Papers, Western Pennsylvania Historical Society, Pittsburgh, Pennsylvania, "Imposing Scene at the Second U.P. Church, Allegheny," *Pittsburgh Gazette*, August 11, 1862.

12. "Presentation to Howe Engineers—Address of Mr. Howe," *Pittsburgh Gazette*, August 21, 1862.

13. Ibid.

14. Ross diary, entry for August 21, 1862.

15. "From Col. Clark's Regiment," *Pittsburgh Gazette*, September 8, 1862.

16. Christian Rhein, "The 123d Pa., A Nine Months Regiment With A Good Bit Of History," *National Tribune*, July 11, 1907.

17. Matthew Borland diary, entry for August 22, 1862. Matthew Borland Papers, Western Pennsylvania Historical Society, Pittsburgh, Pennsylvania.

18. Borland diary, entry for August 29, 1862.

19. Borland diary, entry for August 30, 1862.

20. Borland diary, entry for August 31, 1862.

21. U.S. War Department, *The War of the Rebellion: A Compilation of the Official Records of the Union and Confederate Armies*, vol. 51 (Washington, D.C.: GPO, 1880–1901), 776 (hereinafter referred to as *OR*).

22. *OR* 12, 790.

23. 155th Regimental Association, *Under the Maltese Cross, Antietam to Appomattox: The Loyal Uprising in Western Pennsylvania, 1861–1865: Campaigns 155th Regiment, Narrated by Rank and File* ([Akron, Ohio: Werner], 1910), 737.

24. "Letter from Col. Clark," *Pittsburgh Gazette*, October 8, 1862.

25. D. Porter Marshall, *Company "K," 155th Pennsylvania Volunteers Zouaves* (Pittsburgh: Privately published, 1888), 65–66.

26. *OR* 51, 799.

27. Borland diary, entries for September 3 and September 5, 1862.

28. Borland diary, entry September 8, 1862.

29. R. W. Hemphill to "Father," September 3, 1862, Hemphill Letters, Henry Family Papers, Unites States Army Military History Institute, Carlisle Barracks, Pennsylvania (hereinafter referred to as USAMHI) and September 11, 1862.

30. R. W. Hemphill to "Father," September 11, 1862.

31. "Letter from Col. Clark," *Pittsburgh Gazette*, September 9, 1862.

32. Borland diary, entry for September 13, 1862.

33. The 91st Pennsylvania was a three-year regiment recruited mainly in Philadelphia. It was commanded by Col. Edgar M. Gregory and had been mustered into service on December 4, 1861. The 126th Pennslvania was a nine-month regiment recruited in Franklin and Juniata County. The men were mostly of Scotch-Irish and German descent. The unit was commanded by Col. James G. Elder and was mustered into state service in August of 1862. The 129th Pennsylvania was also a nine-month regiment which was recruited in Schuylkill, Northhampton, and Montgomery Counties. The commander of the regiment was a Mexican War veteran, Col. Jacob Frick. The men were mustered into service in August of 1862. The last unit in this brigade, the 134th Pennsylvania, had previously been brigaded with the 123rd and was also a nine-month unit. The regiment was recruited in Lawrence, Butler, and Beaver Counties and was also mustered into service in August of 1862. The group was originally commanded by Col. Matthew Quay, a future United States senator. Unfortunately, in December of 1862, Colonel Quay was forced to resign after a bout with typhoid fever and Lt. Col. Edward O'Brien commanded the unit for the remainder of the term.

34. The 131st Pennsylvania was a nine-month regiment raised in the Susquehanna Valley. It was mustered into state service on August 16, 1862, and was originally commanded by Colonel Allabach. After his ascension to brigade command, Lt. Col. William B. Shaut commanded the unit. The 133rd Pennsylvania was raised in Cambria, Perry, Bedford, and Somerset Counties. The regiment was fully mustered in on August 15, 1862, and was led by Col. Frank B. Speakman. The majority of the men were reported as being "hardy mountain men" from the Allegheny Mountains. The 155th Pennsylvania was a three-year unit that was recruited at the same time as the 123rd in Pittsburgh. Its colonel, E. J. Allen, was an accomplished author

and a highly respected citizen of Pittsburgh. A strong friendship grew between the 123rd and the 155th during their time in the field. This friendship would never be forgotten, even after the war was over.

35. Carol Reardon, "The Forlorn Hope, Brig. Gen. Andrew A. Humphreys' Pennsylvania Division at Fredericksburg," in *The Fredericksurg Campaign, Decision on the Rappahannock*, ed. Gary Gallagher (Chapel Hill, University of North Carolina Press, 1995), 83–84.

36. Henry H. Humphreys, *Andrew Atkinson Humphreys: A Biography* (Philadelphia: The John C. Winston Company, 1924; reprint, Gaithersburg, Maryland: Ron R. Van Sickle Military Books, 1988), 44–166 (page citations are to the reprint edition).

37. Ibid., 167–168.

38. *OR* 51, 825.

39. Humphreys, *Andrew Atkinson Humphreys*, 168.

40. *OR* 51, 825.

41. *OR* 19, 371 and 370–373. The entire text of General Humphreys' letter can be found in *OR* 19, 370–373.

42. Henry L. Abbott, *Memoir of Andrew Atkinson Humphreys, Read before the National Academy of Science, April 24, 1885* (n.p., 1885), 1.

43. Larry Tagg, *The Generals of Gettysburg: The Leaders of America's Greatest Battle* (Mason City, Iowa: Savas Publishing Co., 1990), 73.

44. Abbott, *Memoir of Andrew Atkinson Humphreys*, 1.

45. Tagg, *The Generals of Gettysburg*, 73.

46. Ted Alexander, *The 126th Pennsylvania* (Shippensburg, Pennsylvania: Beidel Printing House, Inc., 1984), 40.

47. Ross diary, entry for September 14, 1862.

48. 155th Regimental Assn., *Under the Maltese Cross*, 69.

49. Borland diary, entry for September 15, 1862.

50. Ibid.

51. Ross diary, entry for September 15, 1862.

52. Marshall, *Co. "K," 155th Pa. Volunteer Zouaves*, 61.

53. 155th Regimental Assn., *Under the Maltese Cross*, 71.

54. Ibid., 69.

55. *OR* 19, 373.

56. 155th Regimental Assn., *Under the Maltese Cross*, 71.

57. See Borland and Ross diary, entry for September 17, 1862.

58. 155th Regimental Assn., *Under the Maltese Cross*, 73.

59. Rhein, "123D PA," *National Tribune*, July 11, 1907.

60. Ross diary, entry for September 17, 1862.

61. R. W. Hemphill to "Father," October 2, 1862.

62. "Letter from Col. Clark," *Pittsburgh Gazette*, September 30, 1862, and October 8, 1862.

63. "Col. Allen's Regiment, *Pittsburgh Gazette*, October 17, 1862.

64. Borland diary, entry for October 7, 1862.

65. R. W. Hemphill, "Dear Father," October 2, 1862.

66. Borland diary, entry for October 15, 1862.

67. "Letter from Col. Clark," *Pittsburgh Gazette*, September 30, 1862.

68. Ross diary, entry for October 3, 1862.

69. "Letter from Colonel Clark," *Pittsburgh Gazette*, October 8, 1862.

70. The Joshua Chamberlain Papers, Bowdoin College, Brunswick, Maine.

CHAPTER 2
March to Fredericksburg

1. Letter from Lincoln to McClellan, October 24 [25], 1862.

2. Andrew Jackson Hartsock, *Soldier of the Cross: The Civil War Diary and Correspondence of Rev. Andrew Jackson Hartsock*, edited by James C. Duran and Eleanor A. Duran (Manhattan, Kansas: American Military Institute, 1979), 20.

3. Ross diary, entry for October 30, 1862.

4. Hartsock, *Soldier of the Cross*, 20.

5. Ross diary, entry for October 30, 1862.

6. Hartsock, *Soldier of the Cross*, 20.

7. Borland diary, entry for October 30, 1862.

8. Borland diary, entry for October 31, 1862. Private Ross in his diary entry for the second indicates that the regiment marched 20 miles. Private Borland only placed the march at 18 miles.

9. Borland diary, entry for November 6, 1862, and November 7, 1862.

10. Ross diary, entry for November 7, 1862.

11. Borland diary, entry for November 8, 1862.

12. Hartsock, *Soldier of the Cross*, 29.

13. Robert W. Hemphill, "Dear Father," November 9, 1862.

14. 155th Regimental Assn., *Under the Maltese Cross*, 87.

15. "Letter from Colonel Clark," *Pittsburgh Gazette*, October 8, 1862.

16. Ibid.

17. 155th Regimental Assn., *Under the Maltese Cross*, 87.

18. "A Card," *Pittsburgh Gazette*, January 17, 1863.

19. Ibid.

20. Shelby Foote, *The Civil War—Fort Sumter to Perryville* (New York: Vintage Books, 1986), 755.

21. Ibid., 756.

22. Borland diary, entry for November 16, 1862.

23. Ross diary, entry for November 16, 1862.

24. Ross diary, entry for November 17, 1862.

25. Borland diary, entry for November 17, 1862.

26. Ross diary, entry for November 18, 1862.

27. Vorin E. Whan, Jr., *Fiasco at Fredericksburg* (University Park, Pennsylvania: Pennsylvania State University, 1960; reprint, Gathersburg, Maryland: Olde Soldier Books, Inc., 1995), 24–26 (page citations are to the reprint edition).

28. "Army Correspondence—Letter from Col. Clark's Regiment—Religion in Camp—Confidence in the New Commander, etc., etc.", *Pittsburgh Chronicle*, December 3, 1862.

29. Marshall, *Company "K"—155th Pa. Volunteer Zouaves*, 78.

30. Adam Ferguson, Company E, died suddenly on November 26; Henry Harbison of Company A succumbed to typhoid fever on November 29; Samuel T. Harris of Company E died on December 4 and Edward Blake of Company A died in Pittsburgh during this time, but the exact date is unknown. "Army Correspondence," *Pittsburgh Chronicle*, December 3, 1862.

31. Darius N. Couch, "Sumner's Right Grand Division," in *Battles and Leaders of the Civil War*, edited by Robert Underwood Johnson and Clarence Clough Buel, vol. 3 (New York: Century, 1887–1888), 108.

32. Ibid.

33. R. W. Hemphill, "Dear Brother," December 1, 1862.

34. "Letter from Col. Allen's Regiment—Health of Pittsburghers—How Time is Passed in Camp, etc.," *Pittsburgh Chronicle*, December 16, 1862.

35. Borland diary, entry for December 9, 1862.

36. Borland diary, entry for December 10, 1862.

37. Ross diary, entry for December 10, 1862.

38. Whan, *Fiasco at Fredericksburg*, 36.

39. Ibid., 40.

40. Ross diary, entry for December 11, 1862.

41. Hartsock, *Soldier of the Cross*, 37.

42. Thomas Rice, "Fredericksburg Under Fire—All the Imps of Hell Let Loose," *Civil War Times Illustrated* (June 1983): 12.

43. Ibid.

44. Lt. Col. George F. R. Henderson, *The Civil War—A Soldier's View* (Chicago: University of Chicago, 1958), 24–25.

45. Whan, *Fiasco at Fredericksburg*, 51–52.

CHAPTER 3
Battle of Fredericksburg

1. John C. Anderson to "Father, Mother and Sister and the . . .," January 10, 1863, Fredericksburg and Spotsylvania National Military Park (FSNMP), Bound Volume #120.

2. James Longstreet, *From Manassas to Appomattox*, 2d edition (Philadelphia: J. P. Lippincott Co., 1903; reprint, New York: Smithmark Publishers, Inc., 1992), 306 (page citations are to the reprint edition).

3. Ross diary, entry for December 13, 1862.

4. In actuality, three bridges were known to cross the millrace at the time of the battle. Unfortunately, the other two bridges, one at Prussia (now Lafayette Boulevard) and another at the Fredericksburg and Valley Plank Road (now William Street) were of no use to the 123rd when it reached the canal since they were too far north and south of their line of attack. Also, it was reported that at least three temporary planks were thrown across the millrace to help get the troops up the hill. For further discussion see Noel G. Harrison, *Fredericksburg Civil War Sites, Volume Two, December 1862—April 1865*, (Lynchburg, Virginia : H. E. Howard, Inc., 1995), 160–163.

5. Humphreys, *Andrew Atkinson Humphreys*, 174.

6. This was the residence of Alan Stratton and his family. The house was described as a two-story brick structure built in the Greek architectural style. The house still stands on what is now called Little Page Street. Interestingly, most writings talk of the Stratton House but very few mention the Stratton Millwright Shop. The two wooden structures were believed to be a blacksmith shop and a woodworking shop. Both structures were known to have been destroyed by May of 1864. Harrison, *Fredericksburg Civil War Sites*, 174–177.

7. If you want to know more about these structures, see Harrison, *Fredericksburg Civil War Sites*, 123–151.

8. Whan, *Fiasco at Fredericksburg*, 84.

9. Harrison, *Fredericksburg Civil War Sites*, 125.

10. Couch, "Sumner's Right Grand Division," *Battles and Leaders of the Civil War*, vol. 3, 113.

11. Harrison, *Fredericksburg Civil War Sites*, 180; The losses consisted of 89 killed, 904 wounded and 167 captured or missing. Return of Casualties for the Battle of Fredericksburg, *OR* 21: 263.

12. Whan, *Fiasco at Fredericksburg*, 86.

13. *OR* 21, 229; 219 men were killed, 1,584 were wounded, and 229 captured or missing.

14. Report of Brig. Gen. Oliver O. Howard, *OR* 21, 263.

15. Return of Casualties, *OR* 21, 129–142.

16. Report of Orlando B. Willcox, *OR* 21, 312.

17. Return of Casualties, *OR* 21, 129–142.

18. Whan, *Fiasco at Fredericksburg*, 95.

19. Testimony of Gen. Joseph Hooker, Report on the Conduct of the War, pt. I, 667.

20. "Letter from Capt. Drum's Company," *Pittsburgh Gazette*, December 19, 1862.

21. Hartsock, *Soldier of the Cross*, 38.

22. Reardon, "The Forlorn Hope, Brig. Gen. Andrew A. Humphreys' Pennsylvania Division at Fredericksburg," *The Fredericksburg Campaign*, 87; 155th Regimental Assn., *Under the Maltese Cross*, 538.

23. 155th Regimental Assn., *Under the Maltese Cross*, 96.

24. Ibid.

25. Ross diary, entry for December 13, 1862.

26. Rhein, "The 123rd," July 11, 1907.

27. "Army Correspondence," *Pittsburgh Post*, December 27, 1862.

28. Hartsock, *Soldier of the Cross*, 38.

29. Ibid.

30. "Col. Clarke's Regiment," *Pittsburgh Gazette*, December 20, 1862.

31. Report of Brig. Gen. Andrew A. Humphreys, *OR* 33, 430.

32. Couch, "Sumner's Right Grand Divison," *Battles and Leaders of the Civil War*, vol. 3, 115.

33. Borland diary, entry for December 13, 1862.

34. 155th Regimental Assn., *Under the Maltese Cross*, 538–539.

35. Hartsock, *Soldier of the Cross*, 39.

36. S. W. Hill, "Allabach's Brigade. It Went as Near as Any Others to the Deadly Stone Wall at Fredericksburg," *National Tribune*, April 16, 1908.

37. Report on the Conduct of War, Part 1, 667.

38. None of the reports filed by any of the regimental commanders of Allabach's brigade state that their officers were ordered to the front. Further, General Humphreys never indicated in his report that this order was given to Allabach's brigade. He only makes this assertion, in his narrative, after the charge of Allabach's brigade is completed and before the charge of Tyler's brigade begins. See Report of Brig. Gen. Andrew A. Humphreys, *OR* 21, 431.

39. Alexander, *The 126th Pennsylvania*, 133.

40. Frank Arundel, *Anecdotes, Poetry and Incidents of the War: North and South, 1860–1865* (New York: Arundel, 1882), 210.

41. 155th Regimental Assn., *Under the Maltese Cross*, 97.

42. Carswell McClellan, *General Andrew A. Humphreys at Malvern Hill VA.—July 1, 1862 and at Fredericksburg—December 13, 1862—A Memoir* (St. Paul: Privately Published, 1888), 14–15.

43. 155th Regimental Assn., *Under the Maltese Cross*, 539.

44. McClellan, *General Andrew A. Humphreys at Malvern Hill VA.*, 14–15.

45. Hill, "Allabach's Brigade," April 16, 1908.

46. "Letter from Col. Clark," *Pittsburgh Gazette*, December 25, 1862.

47. 155th Regimental Assn., *Under the Maltese Cross*, 539.

48. Report on the Conduct of War, Part 1, p. 667.

49. Alexander, *The 126th Pennsylvania*, 133.

50. Editors of Time-Life Books, *Voices of the Civil War—Fredericksburg* (Alexandria, Virginia: Time-Life, 1998), 123–124.

51. Francis A. Walker, *History of the Second Army Corps in the Army of the Potomac* (New York: Charles Scribner & Sons, 1886), 180.

52. Report of Brig. Gen. Andrew A. Humphreys, *OR* 21, 431.

53. 155th Regimental Assn., 558.

54. Emmanuel Noll, "Allabach's Brigade. It Attacked at Fredericksburg Before Tyler's Brigade and Went Further," *National Tribune*, October 1, 1908.

55. Frederick B. Arner, *Red Tape and Pigeon Hole Generals* (Charlotteville, Virginia: Rockbridge Publishing, 1999), 319–320. Unfortunately for the major, he did not ask Colonel Clark's permission to leave the field. In the weeks after the battle, the major would be court-martialed for his conduct.

56. Noll, "Allabach's Brigade," April 16, 1908.

57. Report of Col. Franklin B. Speakman, *OR* 21, 446.

58. Report of Brig. Gen. Andrew A. Humphreys, *OR* 21, 433.

59. Alexander, *126th Pennsylvania*, 133.

60. Hill, "Allabach's Brigade," April 16, 1908.

61. Report of Col. Peter H. Allabach, *OR* 21, 443.

62. Report of Brig. Gen. Andrew A. Humphreys, *OR* 21, 433.

63. Hill, "Allabach's Brigade," April 16, 1908.

64. John Anderson, FSNMP, Bound Volume #120.

65. "Letter from Capt. Drum's Company," *Pittsburgh Gazette*, December 19, 1862.

66. Hill, "Allabach's Brigade," April 16, 1908.

67. "Letter from Capt. Drum's Company," *Pittsburgh Gazette*, December 19, 1862.

68. 155th Regimental Assn., *Under the Maltese Cross*, 102.

69. *OR* 21, 431.

70. Hill, Allabach's Brigade, April 16, 1908.

71. John Anderson, FSNMP, Bound Volume #120.

72. Hill, Allabach's Brigade, April 16, 1908.

73. Report of Peter H Allabach, *OR* 21, 443–444.

74. Report of Col. John B. Clark, *OR* 21, 444–445.

75. 155th Regimental Assn., *Under the Maltese Cross*, 539.

76. Capt. Robert T. Humes of Company I was wounded in the thigh; Captain Boyd received a slight wound; and Capt. Horatio K. Tyler was wounded slightly in the shoulder. "List of Casualties in Col. Clark's Regiment," *Pittsburgh Gazette*, December 19, 1862.

77. " . . . Second Lieutenant S. D. Karns . . . received a gunshot through the right arm. The First Lieutenant, J. R. Coulter, was killed, while Capt. Humes was shot through the right thigh, the ball penetrating about the joint, and passing entirely through . . . Lieutenant Samuel A. Long of Capt. Drum's company, was ordered to take command." "Col. Clarke's Regiment, *Pittsburgh Gazette*, December 20, 1862.

78. Richard A. Sauers, *Advance the Colors—Pennsylvania Civil War Battle Flags* (Lebanon, Pennsylvania: Sowers Printing Co., 1991), 396.

79. 155th Regimental Assn., *Under the Maltese Cross*, 102.

80. Hill, "Allabach's Brigade," April 16, 1908.

81. "A Soldier's Diary," *Williamsport Gazette*, January 12, 1891.

82. Report of Peter H. Allabach, *OR* 21, 443.

83. Couch, "Sumner's Right Grand Division,"*Battles and Leaders*, vol. 3, 115.

84. Humphreys, *Andrew Atkinson Humphreys*, 178, 432–433.

85. Report of Brig. Gen. Andrew A. Humphreys, *OR* 21, 433.

86. Report of Brig. Gen. Andrew A. Humphreys, *OR* 21, 430. See appendix A.

87. This number is based on the figure given by General Humphreys for the effective strength of the division. No official reports have been found which give the true strength of the regiment for the 13th of December. But the 560 figure is more than likely very close to the actual strength. As previously indicated, Sergeant Bard reported that many were relieved from duty on the day of battle due to illness. Further, on November 26, only 17 days before the battle, a member of the regiment stated that "the number of men . . . fit for duty will not exceed seven hundred." "Army Correspondence," *Pittsburgh Chronicle*, December 3, 1862.

88. Alexander, *The 126th Pennsylvania*, 43.

89. "Allabach's Brigade," October 1, 1908.

90. Arner, *Red Tape and Pigeon-Hole Generals*, 189.

91. Noll, "Allabach's Brigade," October 1, 1908.

92. Hill, "Allabach's Brigade," April 16, 1908.

93. Arner, *Red Tape and Pigeon-Hole Generals*, 191.

94. Report of Brig. Gen. Andrew A. Humphreys, *OR* 21, 432.

95. Report of Col. Peter H. Allabach, *OR* 21, 444.

96. 155th Regimental Assn., *Under the Maltese Cross*, 103–104.

97. Ibid., 104.

98. "Army Correspondence," *Pittsburgh Post*, December 30, 1862.

99. The writer of the poem evidently changed the name of the deceased since no one in the 123rd who was killed was named "Harry." "The Soldier's Return, "*Pittsburgh Gazette*, March 5, 1863.

100. 155th Regimental Assn., *Under the Maltese Cross*, 426.

101. Letter from Col. Clark," *Pittsburgh Gazette*, December 25, 1862.

102. "Army Correspondence," *Pittsburgh Post*, December 27, 1862.

103. Time-Life Books, *Voices of the Civil War—Fredericksburg*, 135.

104. Hartsock, *Soldier of the Cross*, 42.

105. Report of Brig. Gen. Andrew A. Humphreys, *OR* 21, 433.

106. "Letter from Col. Clark," *Pittsburgh Gazette*, December 25, 1862.

107. Hartsock, *Soldier of the Cross*, 44.

108. Ibid.

109. Borland diary, entry for December 15, 1862.

110. Ross diary, entry for December 14, 1862.

111. Rhein, "123d Pa.," July 11, 1907.

112. Borland diary, entry for December 16, 1862.

113. "Letter from Col. Clark," *Pittsburgh Gazette*, December 25, 1862.

114. Borland diary, entry for December 16, 1862.

115. Report on the Conduct of War, pt. 1, 671.

CHAPTER 4
The Aftermath of Fredericksburg

1. See appendix B; Rhein, "The 123d Pa," July 11, 1907.

2. "Letter from Col. Clark," *Pittsburgh Gazette*, December 25, 1862.

3. Report on the Conduct of War, pt. 1, 667.

4. At the time of the dispute, Henry H. Humphreys was a captain in the 15th U.S. Infantry. He had received, during the Civil War, a number of brevets which led to his lieutenant colonel rank. He was stationed at Fort Sheridan, Illinois. Gen. Francis A. Walker was a former member of the II Corps and wrote its history. The debate between Henry Humphreys and General Walker would rage on for nearly four years and would unwittingly draw many former comrades into the fray.

5. Walker, *History of the Second Corps in the Army of the Potomac*, 184.

6. Ibid., 18.

7. Ibid., 18–19.

8. Henry H. Humphreys, *Major General Andrew Atkinson Humphreys: United States Volunteers at Fredericksburg VA., December 13th, 1862 and Farmville, VA., April 17th, 1865* (Chicago: Press of R. E.McCabe & Co., 1896), 23.

9. Ibid.

10. The argument was contained in its regimental history published in 1902.

11. Joseph R. Orwig, *History of the 131st Penna. Volunteers, War 1861–1865* (Williamsport, Pennsylvania: Sun Book and Printing House, 1902), 123.

12. The regimental history was published in 1910 and is probably one of the most extensive histories of a regiment, numbering over 800 pages.

13. 155th Regimental Assn., *Under the Maltese Cross*, 425–426.

14. Report of Col. Peter H. Allabach, *OR* 21, 444.

15. Report on the Conduct of War, pt. 1, 667.

16. "List of Casualties in Col.Clark's Regiment—16 Killed, 115 Wounded and 97 Missing," *Pittsburgh Gazette*, December 19, 1862.

17. Colonel Speakman's statement can be found in his report, *OR* 21, 446. Colonel Allen's statement can be read at *OR* 21, 448.

18. John C. Anderson to "Father, Mother, Sister and the . . ." FSNMP, Bound Volume #120.

19. Samuel P. Bates, *History of Pennsylvania Volunteers, 1861–1865; Prepared in Compliance with Acts of Legislature*, vol. 3 (Harrisburg: B. Singerly, 1870; reprint, Wilmington, North Carolina: Broadfoot Publishing Co., 1994), 188.

20. Alexander, *The 126th Pennsylvania*, 134.

21. "From the Army at Fredericksburg," *Pittsburgh Dispatch*, December 27, 1862.

22. *Confederate Veteran* as quoted in *Under the Maltese Cross*, 102.

23. Humphreys, *Andrew Atkinson Humphreys*, 179.

24. Ibid., 180.

25. "Letter from Col. Clark," *Pittsburgh Gazette*, December 25, 1862.

26. "Army Correspondence," *Pittsburgh Post*, December 27, 1862.

27. Borland diary, entry for December 16, 1862.

28. "Col. Clarke's Regiment," *Pittsburgh Gazette*, December 20, 1862.

29. "Our Boys in the Late Battle," *Pittsburgh Gazette*, December 27, 1862.

30. 155th Regimental Assn., *Under the Maltese Cross*, 142.

31. Report of Col. John B. Clark, *OR* 21, 445.

32. "List of Casualties in Col. Clark's Regiment," *Pittsburgh Gazette*, December 19, 1862.

33. Report of Brig. Gen. Andrew A. Humphreys, *OR* 21, 434.

34. "List of Casualties in Col. Clark's Regiment," *Pittsburgh Gazette*, December 19, 1862.

35. Bates, *Pennsylvania Volunteers*, vol. 4, 73–89.

36. See appendix C.

37. See appendix D.

38. Appendix E.

39. Appendix F lists the casualties for each of the divisions that participated in this charge. The number of casualties, as well as the number of men who participated in the attack, tends to vary, based on what book you are consulting. But these numbers appear to be a fair reflection of the actual casualty figures.

40. The actual number of men in Pickett's attack has never been exactly known. Some estimates have placed the number at 11,000, while others have gone as high as 15,000.

41. Allen's Regiment Not in Fight," *Pittsburgh Chronicle*, December 18, 1862.

42. "List of Casualties in Col. Clark's Regiment," *Pittsburgh Gazette*, December 19, 1862.

43. "Letter from Col. Allen's Regiment—List of Casualties," *Pittsburgh Gazette*, December 19, 1862.

44. "The Late Capt. Boisol," *Pittsburgh Gazette*, January 19, 1862.

45. "The Soldier's Return," *Pittsburgh Gazette*, March 5, 1863.

CHAPTER 5
Rest, Recuperation, and the Mud March

1. Ross diary, entry for December 18,1862, and Borland diary, entry for December 17, 1862.

2. Hartsock, *Soldier of the Cross*, 46.

3. "Army Correspondence," *Pittsburgh Post*, December 27, 1862.

4. Rhein, "The 123d Pa.," July 11, 1907.

5. "Letter from Col. Clark," *Pittsburgh Gazette*, December 29, 1862.

6. "From the 123rd Regiment," *Pittsburgh Gazette*, January 12, 1863.

7. Borland diary, entry for January 1, 1863.

8. Marshall, *Company "K"—155th Pa. Volunteer Zouaves*, 80.

9. Robert W. Hemphill, "Father," December 29, 1862.

10. The following were discharged during this time: Andrew Marks, Co. I, December 20, 1862; Samuel Kuhn, Co. I, December 22, 1862; Jacob Byers, Co. F, December 23, 1862; James Harbison, Co. A, December 28, 1862; James Leitch, Co. E, January 4, 1863; John S. Clark, Co. K, January 10, 1863; Joseph Geyer, Co. K, January 10, 1863; John Quinn, Co. K, January 10, 1863; Charles Schwarberg, Co. G, January 10, 1862; Robert B. Hill, Co. F, January 11, 1863; Wesley Todd, Co. G, January 16, 1863; Robert Sneed, Co. G, January 16, 1863; John Hall, Co. C, January 17, 1863, and Commodore Biddle, Co. E, January 19, 1863.

11. "The Reverse at Fredericksburg," *Harper's Weekly*, December 27, 1862.

12. Gallagher, ed., *The Fredericksburg Campaign*, 186.

13. Ibid.

14. Foote, *The Civil War—A Narrative*, vol. 2, 128.

15. *OR* 21, 977.

16. Ross diary, entry for January 16, 1863, and January 18, 1863.

17. Borland diary, entry for January 21, 1863.

18. Ibid.

19. 155th Regimental Assn., *Under the Maltese Cross*, 113.

20. Alexander, *The 126th Pennsylvania*, 137.

21. 155th Regimental Assn., *Under the Maltese Cross*, 113.

22. Marshall, *Company "K"—155th Pennsylvania Zouaves*, 82.

23. 155th Regimental Assn., *Under the Maltese Cross*, 113.

24. Borland diary, entry for January 24, 1863.

CHAPTER 6
Winter Quarters—Camp Humphreys

1. Borland diary, entry for January 29, 1863.
2. 155th Regimental Assn., *Under the Maltese Cross*, 115.
3. "Letter from Col. Clark," *Pittsburgh Gazette*, February 21, 1863.
4. 155th Regimental Assn., *Under the Maltese Cross*, 120.
5. "Reduced," *Pittsburgh Post*, February 18, 1863.
6. "Letter from Col. Clark," *Pittsburgh Gazette*, February 21, 1863.
7. "The 123rd Regiment," *Pittsburgh Gazette*, March 7, 1863.
8. Robert W. Hemphill, "Dear Father," February 6, 1863.
9. 155th Regimental Assn., *Under the Maltese Cross*, 123–124.
10. The five who died from disease were: William Tweedy, Company I, February 7, 1863; Robert Bard, Company H, February 11, 1863; George Chambers, Company F, February 18, 1863; John C. Silvis, Company I, February 28, 1863; and William Smalley, Company I, February 28, 1863.

    The five who were discharged were James Hays, Company K, February 3, 1863; James O. Brown, Company H, February 6, 1863; Charles Albrite, Company D, February 13, 1863; Ebenezer Johnston, Company E, February 14, 1863; and William Morrow, February 17, 1863.
11. The four who died were John H. Patterson, Company F, March 5, 1863; James Stevenson, Company C, March 7, 1863; Lieutenant Eli Hemphill, Company F, March 21, 1863; and Robert McCausland, Company G, March 27, 1863.
12. John Sands of Company F died on April 15, 1863. Henry Agnew of Company G was discharged on April 7, 1863.
13. Robert W. Hemphill, "Dear Father," March 23, 1863. Bates reports that Captain Boyd was discharged on the March 7 date.
14. Borland diary, entry for April 19, 1863.
15. Robert W. Hemphill, "Dear Father," April 14, 1863.

CHAPTER 7
Battle of Chancellorsville

1. Ross diary, entry for April 14, 1863.
2. *OR* 25, pt. 1: 545.
3. Humphreys, *Andrew Atkinson Humphreys*, 183.
4. Borland diary, entry for April 15, 1863.
5. Ross diary, entry for April 27, 1863.
6. *OR* 25, pt. 1: 505.
7. Marshall, *Company "K"—155th Pa. Volunteer Zouaves*, 93.
8. *OR* 25, pt. 1: 545.
9. Ross diary, entry for April 29, 1863.
10. 155th Regimental Assn., *Under the Maltese Cross*, 129.
11. Ibid.
12. Rhein, *The 123d Pa.*, July 11, 1907.
13. *OR* 25, pt. 1: 546.
14. Marshall, *Company "K"—155th Pa. Volunteer Zouaves*, 94.
15. *OR* 25, pt. 1: 546.
16. Ross diary, entry for May 1, 1863.
17. Marshall, *Company "K"—155th Pa. Volunteer Zouaves*, 95.

18. *OR* 25, pt. 1: 507.

19. John Bigelow, Jr., *The Campaign for Chancellorsville* (New Haven: Yale University, 1910), 254.

20. Ibid., 477–478n.

21. Hartsock, *Soldier of the Cross*, 97.

22. *OR* 25, pt. 1: 509.

23. Hartsock, *Soldier of the Cross*, 97.

24. Ross diary, entry for May 2, 1863.

25. *OR* 25, pt. 1: 546.

26. Hartsock, *Soldier of the Cross*, 98.

27. Marshall, *Company "K"—155th Pa. Volunteers Zouaves*, 97.

28. 155th Regimental Assn., *Under the Maltese Cross*, 132.

29. Marshall, *Company "K"—155th Pa. Volunteer Zouaves*, 97.

30. *OR* 25, pt. 1: 941.

31. William Shaw Stewart, FSNMP, Bound Volume #152. Another assistant surgeon, John S. Angle, was dishonorably discharged from the regiment in January of 1863 for being absent without leave. Assistant Surgeon Stewart was sent to the regiment on March 25, 1863, only 13 days after receiving his medical degree. Interestingly, after the regiment was discharged, Surgeon Stewart was reassigned to the 83rd Pennsylvania but was on detached duty with the 20th Maine when it made its heroic stand on Little Round Top in July of 1863.

32. Ross diary, entry for May 2, 1863.

33. Marshall, *Company "K"—155th Pa. Volunteer Zouaves*, 95–96.

34. *OR* 25, pt. 1: 555, 507.

35. Ibid.

36. Samuel P. Bates, "Hooker's Comments on Chancellorsville," Robert Underwood Johnson and Clarence Clough Buel, eds., *Battles and Leaders of the Civil War*, vol. 3 (New York: Century, 1887–1888), 221.

37. "The 123rd Regiment Denouncing Copperheads—Bald Lies in the Tory Organs at Harrisburg and Pittsburgh," *Pittsburgh Gazette*, May 16, 1863.

38. Ibid.

39. "Enthusiastic Reception of Colonel Clark's Regiment—A Cordial Welcome Home," *Pittsburgh Gazette*, May 18, 1863.

40. Marshall, *Company "K"—155th Pa. Volunteer Zouaves*, 99–100.

41. Report of Brig. Gen. Erastus B. Tyler, *OR* 25, pt. 1: 551.

42. 155th Regimental Assn., *Under the Maltese Cross*, 133.

43. Marshall, *Company "K"—155th Pa. Volunteer Zouaves*, 96.

44. 155th Regimental Assn., *Under the Maltese Cross*, 136.

45. Report of Brig. Gen. Andrew A. Humphreys, *OR* 25, pt. 1: 548.

46. Report of Col. Peter H. Allabach, *OR* 25, pt. 1: 548.

47. 155th Regimental Assn., *Under the Maltese Cross*, 137–138.

48. Report of Col. Peter H. Allabach, *OR* 25, pt. 1: 548.

49. Ross diary, entry for May 3, 1863.

50. Rhein, "The 123rd PA., July 11, 1907.

51. Ross diary, entry for May 3, 1863.

52. Bates, *Pennsylvania Volunteers*, vol. 4, 73.

53. Report of Brig. Gen. Andrew A. Humphreys, *OR* 25, pt. 1: 548.

54. Ross diary, entry for May 4, 1863. The entry itself is titled "Monday May 5, 1863." Since Monday was clearly May 4, it is the writer's belief that the diary entry was erroneously captioned. Further, the events in the diary coincide with the events recorded by others for May 4.

55. Ross diary, entry for May 5, 1863.

56. Report of Brig. Gen. Andrew A. Humphreys, *OR* 25, pt. 1: 548.

57. Ross diary, entry for May 5, 1863.

58. Marshall, *Company "K"—155th Pa. Volunteer Zouaves*, 97.

59. Ross diary, entry for May 5, 1863.

60. Report of Andrew A. Humphreys, *OR* 25, pt. 1: 548.

61. Ross diary, entry for May 5, 1863.

62. Report of Brig. Gen. Andrew A. Humphreys, *OR* 25, pt. 1: 548.

63. Report of Brig. Gen. Andrew A. Humphreys, *OR* 25, pt. 1: 549.

CHAPTER 8
Coming Home

1. 155th Regimental Assn., *Under the Maltese Cross*, 144.

2. Report of Brig. Gen. Andrew A. Humphreys, *OR* 25, pt. 1: 549.

3. 155th Regimental Assn., *Under the Maltese Cross*, 145.

4. "From the 123d Regiment," *Pittsburgh Gazette*, May 14, 1863.

5. "A Member of the 123d Regiment Killed," *Pittsburgh Gazette*, May 14, 1863.

6. "The Death of Andrew McKain," *Pittsburgh Gazette*, May 16, 1863.

7. "Enthusiastic Reception for Col. Clark's Regiment," *Pittsburgh Gazette*, May 18, 1863.

8. "Reception of Col. Clark and the 123d Regiment," *Pittsburgh Post*, May 18, 1863.

9. "Enthusiastic Reception of Colonel Clark's Regiment," *Pittsburgh Gazette*, May 18, 1863.

10. "Reception of Col. Clark," *Pittsburgh Gazette*, May 18, 1863.

11. Ibid.

12. Ibid.

13. Initially, Captain Tyler recruited an artillery battery that eventually became known as Tyler's Independent Battery. In July of 1864, he was elected as the major of the 193rd Pennsylvania. He completed his military duty as a captain in the 61st Pennsylvania, a hard-fought regiment primarily from Pittsburgh.

14. Lieutenant Bartley was an expert in explosives and was in charge of blowing up the bridges leading to Richmond. After the raid failed, he evaded capture for some time but was ultimately apprehended by the enemy and imprisoned in Libby Prison.

15. Sergeant Taggart, upon his arrival home, almost immediately entered the United Presbyterian Seminary in Allegheny. But in the spring of 1864, he recruited and was appointed captain of a new company in the 116th Pennsylvania Volunteers. Unfortunately, on August 25, 1864, while the captain was in command of the regiment, he was struck by a sharpshooter's bullet. He died on the field, but the body of the 24-year-old seminarian was returned to Pittsburgh for burial.

16. 155th Regimental Assn., *Under the Maltese Cross*, 706.

17. *Dedication of Monument Erected to Commemorate The Charge of General Humphreys' Division* (Philadelphia: J. P. Lippincott, 1908), 19.

18. Ibid.

19. Donald Pfanz, *Fredericksburg and Spotsylvania National Military Park Monument Guide*, 72–82.

BIBLIOGRAPHY

Books and Articles

155th Regimental Association. *Under the Maltese Cross, Antietam to Appomattox: The Loyal Uprising in Western Pennsylvania, 1861-1865; Campaigns of the 155th Regiment, Narrated by Rank and File.* Akron: Werner, 1910.

Abbott, Henry L. *Memoir of Andrew Atkinson Humphreys, Read before the National Academy of Science, April 24, 1885* (n.p., 1885).

Alexander, Ted. *The 126th Pennsylvania.* Shippensburg, Pennsylvania: Beidel Printing House, Inc., 1984.

Allegheny Centennial Committee. *Story of Old Allegheny.* Pittsburgh: Hebrick and Held Printing Co., 1941.

Arner, Frederick B. *Red Tape and Pigeon Hole Generals.* Charlottesville, Virginia: Rockbridge Publishing, 1999.

Arundel, Frank. *Anecdotes, Poetry and Incidents of the War: North and South, 1860-1865.* New York: Arundel, 1882.

Bates, Samuel P. *History of Pennsylvania Volunteers, 1861-1865; Prepared in Compliance with Acts of the Legislature.* Vol. 4. Harrisburg: B. Singerly, 1870; reprint, Wilmington, North Carolina: Broadfoot Publishing Company, 1994.

Bigelow, John, Jr. *The Campaign for Chancellorsville.* New Haven, Connecticut: Yale University, 1910.

Cullen, Joseph P. *The Battle for Chancellorsville.* Harrisburg: Eastern Acorn Press, 1981.

Foote, Shelby. *The Civil War—A Narrative—Fort Sumter to Perryville.* New York: Vintage Books, 1986.

170

Frassanito, William A. *Antietam—The Photographic Legacy of America's Bloodiest Day*. New York: Simon and Schuster, 1978.

Fredericksburg Battlefield Memorial Commission. *Dedication of Monument Erected by Pennsylvania to Commemorate the Charge of Humphreys' Division*. Philadelphia: J. B. Lippincott Company, 1908.

Furgeson, Ernest B. *Chancellorsville 1863—The Souls of the Brave*. New York: Alfred A. Knopf, 1992.

Gallagher, Gary, ed. *The Fredericksburg Campaign: Decision on the Rappahannock*. Chapel Hill: University of North Carolina Press, 1995.

Golay, Michael. *To Gettysburg and Beyond—The Parallel Lives of Joshua Chamberlain and Edward Porter Alexander*. New York: Crown Publishers, 1994.

Harrison, Noel G. *Fredericksburg Civil War Sites, Volume Two, December 1862–April 1865*. Lynchburg, Virginia: H. E. Howard Inc., 1995.

Henderson, Lt. Col. George F. R. *The Civil War—A Soldier's View*. Chicago: University of Chicago, 1958.

Hill, S. W. "Allabach's Brigade It Went as Near as Any Others to the Deadly Stone Wall at Fredericksburg." *National Tribune*, April 10, 1908.

Humphreys, Henry H. *Andrew Atkinson Humphreys, A Biography*. Philadelphia: The John C. Winston Company, 1924; reprint, Gaithersburg, Maryland: Ron R. Van Sickle Military Books, 1988.

———. *Major General Andrew Atkinson Humphreys—United States Volunteers at Fredericksburg VA., December 13th, 1862 and Farmville, VA., April 7th, 1865*. Chicago: Press of R. E. McCabe & Co, 1896.

Johnson, Robert Underwood, and Clarence Clough Buel, ed. *Battles and Leaders of the Civil War*. Vol. 3, *Sumner's Right Grand Division* by Darius N. Couch. New York: Century, 1887-1888.

Longstreet, James. *From Manassas to Appomattox*, 2d ed. Philadelphia: J. P. Lippincott Co., 1903; reprint, New York: Smithmark Publishing Inc., 1992.

Love, W. A., and W. H. Hartzell. *Organization of the Military of Allegheny County*. Pittsburgh: Privately published, 1862.

Luvaas, Jay, and Harold W. Nelson, ed. *The U.S. Army War College Guide to the Battles of Chancellorsville and Fredericksburg*. New York: Harper & Row, 1988.

Marshall, D. P. *Company "K," The 155th Pa. Volunteer Zouaves*. Pittsburgh: Privately published, 1888.

McClellan, Carswell. *General Andrew A. Humphreys at Malvern Hill VA.—July 1, 1862 and Fredericksburg—December 13, 1862—A Memoir*. St. Paul, Minnesota: Privately published, 1888.

McClellan, George B. *Army of the Potomac*. Washington, D.C.: Government Printing Office ,1864.

McPherson, James M. *Battle Cry of Freedom—The Civil War Era*. New York: Ballantine, 1989.

Mulholland, St. Clair A. *The Story of the 116th Regiment Pennsylvania Volunteers in the War of the Rebellion*. Edited by Lawrence Frederick Kohl. New York: Fordham Press, 1996.

Noll, Emmanuel. "Allabach's Brigade. It Attacked at Fredericksburg Before Tyler's Brigade and Went Further." *National Tribune*, October 1, 1908.

Priest, John Michael. *Antietam—The Soldiers' Battle*. New York: Oxford University Press, 1989.

Rhein, Christian. "The 123d PA., A Nine Months Regiment With A Good Bit of History." *National Tribune*, July 11, 1907.

Rice, Thomas. "Fredericksburg Under Fire—All the Imps of Hell Let Loose." *Civil War Times Illustrated*, June 1983.

Schildt, John W. *Four Days in October*. Chewsville, Maryland: Privately published, 1978.

Sears, Stephen. *To the Gates of Richmond—The Peninsula Campaign*. New York: Ticknor and Fields, 1992.

Sifalkis, Stewart. *Who Was Who in the Civil War*. New York: Facts on File Publications, 1988.

Stackpole, Edward J. *The Fredericksburg Campaign*. Harrisburg: Stackpole Books, 1991.

Stewart, George R., *Pickett's Charge—A Microhistory of the Final Attack at Gettysburg, July 3, 1863*. Boston: Houghton Mifflin Company, 1959.

Tagg, Larry. *The Generals of Gettysburg: The Leaders of America's Greatest Battle*. Mason City, Iowa: Savas Publishing Co., 1990.

Time-Life Books. *Voices of the Civil War—Fredericksburg*. Alexandria: Time-Life, 1998.

United States. *War of the Rebellion: A Compilation of the Official Records of the Union and Confederate Armies*. Washington, D.C.: Government Printing Office, 1889.

Walker, Francis A. *History of the Second Army Corps in the Army of the Potomac*. New York: Charles Scribner & Sons, 1886.

Wallace, Willard M. *Soul of the Lion—A Biography of Joshua L. Chamberlain*. New York: Thomas Nelson and Sons, 1960; reprint, Gettysburg, Pennsylvania: Stan Clark Military Books, 1991.

Warner, Ezra J. *Generals in Blue: Lives of the Union Commanders*. Baton Rouge: Louisiana State University Press, 1964.

Whan, Vorin E. *Fiasco at Fredericksburg*. University Park, Pennsylvania: Pennsylvania State University, 1960; reprint, Gaithersburg, Maryland: Olde Soldier Books Inc., 1995.

Newspapers

Harper's Weekly, December 27, 1862.

Pittsburgh Chronicle, August 1862–May 1863.

Pittsburgh Daily Gazette, August 1862–May 1863.

Pittsburgh Gazette, August 1862–May 1863.

Pittsburgh Post, August 1862–May 1863.

Williamsport Gazette, January 12, 1891.

Diaries, Letters and Other Sources

Fredericksburg and Spotsylvania National Military Park (FSNMP)

Bound Volume #120—John C. Anderson Letter

Bound Volume #152—William Shaw Stewart Journal

Hartsock, Andrew Jackson. *Soldier of the Cross: The Civil War Diary and Correspondence of Rev. Andrew Jackson Hartsock*. Edited by James C. Duram and Eleanor A. Duram. Manhattan, Kansas: American Military Institute, 1979.

Letter from Lincoln to McClellan, October 24 [25], 1862.

National Archives, Washington, D.C.

> Civil War Soldiers' Service and Pension Records
>
> 123rd Pennsylvania Muster Rolls

Personal Collection

> Letter from Henry R. Bowman to "Cousin and fellow soldier"
>
> Letter from P. M. Galbreth, "Camp near Fort Blinker"
>
> Photographs of brigade and regiment
>
> Song sheet, "Col. Clark's Grand Triumphant March"

Pfanz, Donald. *Fredericksburg and Spotsylvania National Military Park Monument Guide.*

United States Army Military Institute

> Hemphill Civil War Letters—Henry Family Papers
>
> Photographs of regimental members

Western Pennsylvania Historical Society

> James B. Ross Diary
>
> Matthew H. Borland Diary

INDEX

First names were given when known.

A

Adams, David E., 4, 7, 13

Allabach, Peter Hollingshead, 18, 20, 25, 35, 87–88, 112; appointment brigade commander, 15–16; brigade alignment—Fredericksburg, 68–69; brigade's fitness for march to Antietam, 21; Chancellorsville, Battle of, 121–135; charge—Marye's Heights, 71–77, 79, 90; later years, 146; march to Fredericksburg, 63; report—Battle of Fredericksburg, 74

Allegheny City, Pa., xi, 2–3, 9, 37, 86, 89, 96–97, 141, 142, 148

Allen, Edward J., 69, 75, 79, 80, 90, 93

Anderson, John C., 52, 75

Antietam, Battle of, xii, 25–27, 33

Appomattox, 96

Army of Northern Virginia, 12, 27

Army of the Potomac, x, 14, 20, 37, 104, 111

Army of Virginia, 12

B

Banks' Ford, Va., 104, 121–122

Bard, R. W., 63

Bartley, Reuben, 146

Bell, John S., 13, 147

Bennett, David A., 28

Bigler, William, 15

Boisol, Daniel, 97–98

Boonsboro, Md., 26

Borland, Matthew H., 30, 99, 100, 108, 116; entry into Washington, 11; Fredericksburg, Battle of, 84–85, 93; march to Fredericksburg, 36, 42, 47; march to Antietam, 23; Mud March, 105–106; time in Sharpsburg, Md., 29, 33; view of retreat—Second Manassas, 12, 14, 17

Boyd, John, 113

Brackenridge, L., 64, 81, 93, 99

Bradley, John, 13

Brompton House, Va., 55, 58

Buckingham, Catherinus P., 40

Burkhardt, Gottlieb, 101

Burnside, Ambrose E., 40, 44, 104; appointment to command—Army of the Potomac, 40–41; abandonment of battle plan—Fredericksburg, 50, 54; criticism of battle plan, 46–47; Mud March, 104–107; plan of attack—Fredericksburg, 45–46; problem—pontoons, 43, 48; resignation, 104

Butterfield, Daniel, 41

C

Caldwell, James, 30

Caldwell, William, 101

Campbell, Henry C., 28

Camp Curtin, Pa., 9

Camp Humphreys, Va., 108–110

Camp McAuley, Md., 27

Camp Stanton, Va., 11

Carson, Alexander, 81, 112–113

Casey, Silas, 20

Center Grand Division, 41, 42, 45, 50

Chamberlain, Joshua L., 31

Chancellor House, Va., 123, 126

Chandler House, Va., 126

Chancellorsville, Battle of, 121–135; aftermath, 132, 135; plan of attack, 116–117; retreat, 131, 135–136

Chantilly, Va., 15

Chapman, H. L., 84

Childs, James H., 26

Clark, John Barr, 9, 18, 22, 87, 114; acting brigade commander, 112–113; administering to wounded—Antietam, 30–31; arrival at Antietam,

175

W